CONTENTS.

◆

GENERAL STATISTICAL INFORMATION ABOUT LONDON.

GUIDE TO CHIEF PLACES OF INTEREST AND AMUSEMENT, &c.

ATLAS.

GENERAL INDEX TO STREETS, &c.

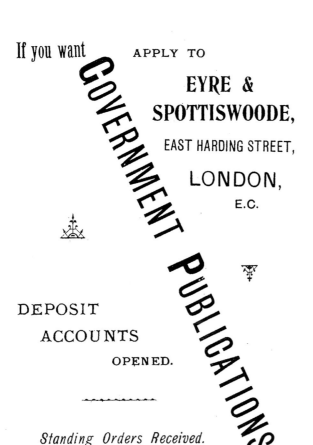

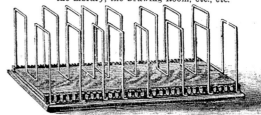

Guide to London

—•—◆—•—

AREA AND POPULATION, 1891.

	Area in Sq. Miles.	Population.
London, within the Registrar-General's Tables of Mortality, ...	116¼	4,211,056
Administrative County of London, ...	118	4,231,431
London School Board District, ...	118	4,231,431
Metropolitan Parliamentary Boroughs, ...	118	4,231,431
The "Greater London" of the Registrar-General's Weekly Return,	684	5,633,332
Consisting of—		
(a) Metropolitan Police District, ...	683	5,595,638
(b) City of London, within the Municipal and Parliamentary limits	1	37,694

The figures for the City represent the *night* population; during the business hours of the day it rises to over 1,000,000.

The population of London in 1801 was 958,863; in 1811, 1,138,815; in 1821, 1,378,947; in 1831, 1,164,994; in 1841, 1,948,369; in 1851, 2,362,236; in 1861, 2,803,989; in 1871, 3,254,260; in 1881, 3,816,483; in 1891, 4,231,431. The annual rate of increase of population since 1801 has thus been about 36,000, and during the last decennial period about 40,000 persons against 56,000 in the previous period, 1871-81.

Parliamentary.—London is divided into 28 electoral divisions, and returns 61 members to the House of Commons. London University also returns 1 member.

Under the Local Government (England and Wales) Act 1888, London is an administrative county, which returns a total of 118 members to the County Council, or double the number of members returned by the Parliamentary boroughs in the Metropolis.

Chronology.—London destroyed by Boadicea, A.D. 61; rebuilt by Theodosius about 306; ravaged by plague, 644; burnt, 798 and 801; made the capital by King Alfred, 893; made a mint town by Athelstane in 925; burnt, 1077, and again in 1136; first mayor appointed, 1190; wasted by plague, 1349 and 1369; scene of Wat Tyler's rebellion, 1381; first lighted by lanterns, 1416; scene of Jack Cade's rebellion, 1450, also date of first lord mayor's show; visited by plague, 1500, 1525, and 1548; houses first built of brick, 1470; Lady Jane Grey appeared in the city, 1553; visited by Elizabeth, 1570; by James I. in 1603; first newspaper published, 1622; first hackney coach appeared, 1634; coal first used 1640; Charles I. beheaded at Whitehall, 1649; visited by Cromwell, 1651; ravaged by great plague, 1664-66; nearly destroyed by fire, 1666; G.P.O. established, 1711; Gordon riots took place, 1780; first canal opened, 1801; cabs first in use, 1820; New London Bridge opened, 1831; first Great World's Exhibition held, 1851; great fire in Tooley Street, 1861; second great Exhibition, 1862; great explosion of gunpowder in Erith Marshes, 1864. Tower Bridge, opened 1894.

ART AND PICTURE GALLERIES.

Agnew's New Art Gallery, 39b Old Bond Street, Piccadilly.—1s., including Cat. Bb 7

Armourers' Hall (a collection of Arms, &c.), Coleman Street.—Daily, on application. Gratuity .. ..

Bridgwater House, Cleveland Place, Green Park.—Magnificent collection of Paintings of the Earl of Ellesmere. On Mondays, Tuesdays, Thursdays, and Fridays, 10-4, by card, to be had from Mr Mitchell, Old Bond Street, or Mr Smith, 137 New Bond Street .. .. Bc 7

British Art Gallery, Grosvenor Road .. .. · .. Ab 13

Cobham Hall, near Gravesend.—Magnificent collection of Paintings. Shown on Fridays, 11-4, by ticket obtained at Caddell's Library, King Street, Gravesend.

Doré Gallery, 35 New Bond Street.—Daily, 10 to 6. 1s. .. .. .: .. Bb 7

Dudley Gallery, Egyptian Hall, Piccadilly.—Admission, 1s. .. .. ..

Dulwich Gallery, near Railway Station, North Dulwich (from London Bridge, Ludgate Hill, or Victoria).—Daily, 10-5, April to October; 10-4, November to March. Free .. ..

French Gallery, 120 Pall Mall.—Admission, 1s.	Bb	7
Grosvenor Gallery, 137 New Bond Street.—Admission, 1s.	Ab	7
Hanover Gallery, 47 New Bond Street, W.	Aa	7
Long Gallery, 168 New Bond Street.—Admission, 1s.	Bb	7
National Gallery, Trafalgar Square.—Monday, Tuesday, Wednesday, and Saturday, 10-4, 5, or 6. Free. Closed during October	Cb	7
National Portrait Gallery, St. Martin's Place, Charing Cross	Cb	7
New Gallery, Regent Street	Bb	7
Raphael Gallery, 4 Cockspur Street.—Open 10 to 6. 1s.	Cb	7
Royal Academy, Burlington House, Piccadilly.—Exhibition of Paintings, May to July. Admission, 1s. ; evening, 6d.	Bb	7
Royal Institute of Painters in Water Colours, Piccadilly, W.—April to July, 1s.	Bb	7
Royal Society of Painters in Water Colours, 5a Pall Mall, E.—Admission, 1s. Open for three months. The April and December exhibitions are confined to Associates and Members	Bc	7
Society of British Artists, 6 Suffolk Street.—Admission, 1s.		

MUSEUMS. *

Antiquaries (*Museum of Society of*), Burlington House.—Daily, 10-4; Saturdays, 10-2. Closed in September. On application to Secretary	Bb	7
Architectural Museum, 18 Tufton Street, Dean's Yard, Westminster.—Open daily, free, from 10-4; Saturdays to 8	Cd	7
Arts, Society of, John Street, Adelphi.—Open free daily, from 10-4, except on Wednesdays and Saturdays	Cb	7
Bethnal Green Museum, near Victoria Park.—Open free on Mondays, Thursdays, and Saturdays from 10 a.m. to 10 p.m.; on Tuesdays and Fridays free, and on Wednesdays on payment of 6d. each person, from 10 to 4, 5, or 6 p.m., according to season	Aa	14
British Museum.—Free. The hours of admission are from 10 all the year round, in January, February, November, December, till 4; March, April, September, October, till 5; and May to August, till 6. On Monday and Saturday, from May 1st to the middle of July, till 8; and onwards to the end of August till 7. The *Reading Room* is open daily from 9, September to April inclusive, till 8; and May to August, till 7	Ca	8
British Museum of Natural History.—The departments of Zoology, Botany, Geology, and Mineralogy, are now in Cromwell Road, S. Kensington. Open from 10 till dusk. On Mondays and Saturdays, May 1 to July 15, open till 8, and July 16 to August 31, till 7. Free	Cd	11
City Museum, Guildhall.—Antiquities, &c. Daily, 10 to 4 or 5	Bb	6
Entomological Museum, 12 Bedford Row.—Mondays, 2-7, on application to Secretary of Entomological Society	Dc	8
Geological Museum, Jermyn Street.—Monday and Saturday, 10-10; Tuesday, Wednesday, and Thursday, 10 to 4 or 5. Closed 10th August to 10th September. Free	Bb	7
Guy's Hospital.—Anatomical Museum, daily, 10-4, on application. (Professional men alone admitted.) See *Hospitals*	Bd	6
India Museum, South Kensington.—Daily, 10-4. Free all the week	Cc	11
King's College, next to Somerset House, Strand.—Museum. Daily, 10-4; Saturday, 10-2, on application	Db	7
London Missionary Society's Museum, 14 Bloomfield Street, Finsbury.—Daily, 10-4; Saturday, 10-2	Cb	6
Museum of Building Appliances, 9 Conduit Street, Regent Street (the property of a Society of Architects.)—Daily, 10-5, on application	Bb	7
Patent Museum, adjoins South Kensington Museum.—Daily, 10-5, free	Cc	11
Saint Bartholomew's Hospital, Smithfield.—Anatomical Museum. Daily, 10-4, Thursday excepted. Also paintings by Hogarth. On application	Ab	6
Soane's Museum, 13 Lincoln's Inn Fields.—Free, on application, on Tuesdays and Thursdays in February and March, and on Tuesdays, Wednesdays, Thursdays, and Fridays, during remainder of year, from 11 till 5	Dc	8

* Some of the National Museums and Galleries are also open at certain hours on Sunday.

South Kensington.—Open daily from 10-10, free on Mondays, Tuesdays, and Saturdays; other days from 10 to 4, 5, or 6, on payment of 6d. .. .. .. Cc **11**

Surgeons' Museum, Lincoln's Inn Fields.—Monday, Tuesday, Wednesday, and Thursday, 12-5. Closed during September. By order of a Member of the Royal College of Surgeons, or by application at Museum .. .. Dc **8**

United Service Museum, Whitehall.—Daily, 6d. (April to Sept., 11-6; Oct. to March, 11-4). On Wednesdays by Member's ticket only .. .. Cc **7**

University College, Gower Street.—Flaxman Museum. Saturday, 10-4, from May to August. On application to Gatekeeper .. .. Bb **8**

PUBLIC BUILDINGS, &c.

Achilles Monument, Hyde Park.—It was cast from cannon taken in the Peninsular War and at Waterloo .. .. Dc **11**

Admiralty. The Offices are in Whitehall.—Hours, 10-5 .. .. .. Cc **7**

Albert Memorial, Hyde Park .. .. Cc **11**

Bank of England, Threadneedle Street.—Public rooms daily, 10-4; Saturdays, 10-2. Vaults, &c., by order of a Director .. .. Bb **6**

Buckingham Palace, St James's Park.—London residence of the Queen. Admission to the Royal stables may be obtained by an order from the Master of the Horse .. .. Bc **7**

Christ's Hospital, Newgate Street.—The paintings are shown daily, 9.30-6, on making written application to the Secretary .. .. Ab **6**

Clarence House, on W. side of St James's Palace, is the town residence of the Duke of Edinburgh .. .. Bc **7**

Cleopatra's Needle, Victoria Embankment .. .. Db **7**

Coal Exchange, Lower Thames Street.—Busiest time on Monday, Wednesday, and Friday, about 1 p.m. The Roman Bath is shown on Tuesday, Thursday, or Saturday, 12-2; gratuity .. .. Cc **6**

Corn Exchange, Mark Lane.—Market days, Monday, Wednesday, and Friday; 11-3 .. .. Cc **6**

Custom House, Lower Thames Street.—Admission to Long Room daily, 10-4 Cc **6**

Cutlers' Hall, Warwick Lane .. ..

Duke of York's Column, Carlton House Gardens.—Admission, 6d. .. .. Bc **7**

Exeter Hall, Strand.—May meetings held here of various religious societies .. Db **7**

Fishmongers' Hall, London Bridge.—Daily .. .. Bc **6**

Foreign and **India Offices,** Downing Street.—Fridays, 12-3, on application to Doorkeeper .. .. Cc **7**

General Post Office, St Martin's-le-Grand .. .. Bb **6**

Goldsmiths' Hall, Foster Lane, behind General Post Office.—Daily, 10-4; Saturdays, 10-2. Written application to Secretary of Company. Gratuity .. Bb **6**

Gordon Monument, Trafalgar Square .. ..

Guildhall.—Daily, 8-5; Museum, 10-4 or 5; Free Library, 9-9 .. .. Bb **6**

Horticultural Society's Gardens, South Kensington.—Daily, 9 to sunset. Admission, 1s.; Mondays, 6d. A band plays on Saturday afternoons .. .. Cd **11**

Houses of Parliament, Westminster.—By ticket obtainable at the Lord Chamberlain's Office in the Victoria Tower, the houses may be viewed on Saturdays, *free*, from 10-4. A member's order is required to admit strangers during the debates .. .. Cc **7**

Imperial Institute, South Kensington.—Open free to the public, Mondays, Tuesdays, and Thursdays, from 10.30 till 3. Admission after 3.30, 1s. On Saturdays, from 12 till 10.30, 6d.; Children, 3d. Other days, by order from Fellows. Band plays from 3.30 to 6, and from 8 to 10.30 .. .. Cd **11**

Kensington Palace, Hyde Park.—Birthplace of Her Majesty Queen Victoria.. Cc **11**

Lambeth Palace.—Town residence of the Archbishop of Canterbury. By permission of the Archbishop's Chaplain. Library, open daily, 10-4, and during sittings of Court of Arches .. .. Dd **7**

Mansion House.—The official residence of the Lord Mayor, with so-called Egyptian Hall. On application.. .. .. Bc **6**

Marlborough House, on E. side of St James's Palace, is the town residence
of the Prince of Wales ..   ..   Bc **7**
Memorial Hall, Farringdon Street ..   ..   Ab **6**
Monument, Fish Street Hill.—Erected in commemoration of the Great Fire
of 1666. Daily, Sundays excepted. Admission, 3d. ..   ..   Cc **6**
Nelson Column, Trafalgar Square, 145 feet in height ..   ..   Cb **7**
People's Palace, Mile End Road, Bow ..   ..   Dd **9**
Public Record Office, Fetter Lane ..   ..   Dc **8**
Royal Courts of Justice, Strand,—Open free during the sittings ..   ..   ..   Da **7**
Royal Exchange, Cornhill ..   ..   Cc **6**
Royal Mint, Tower Hill.—Admission on written application to Deputy Master Dc **6**
St. James's Palace, where the Queen and Prince Albert were married ..   Bc **7**
St. Paul's Cathedral.—On Week-days, 7.45 to dusk. Divine service at 8, 9.45,
and 3.15. Area, free. Whispering and Golden Galleries, 6d. ; Ball, 1s. 6d. (not
worth it) ; Library, Bell, and Geometrical Staircase, 6d. ; Clock, 2d. ; Crypt, 6d... Ab **6**
Somerset House, Strand ..   ..   Db **7**
Temple Bar Memorial, Fleet Street ..   ..   Da **7**
Tower of London, containing regalia, &c. Mondays and Saturdays, *free ;*
other four days, 1s. Armouries, 6d. ; Jewels, 6d. ..   ..   Cc **6**
Tower Bridge.—Opened 1894. Cost £750,000 ..   ..   Cc **6**
Trinity House, Tower Hill.—Admission by ticket, obtainable from the Secretary Cc **6**
Westminster Abbey.—Free ; Nave and Cloisters, 6d. ..   ..   Cc **7**
Whitehall Chapel.—Open on Sundays, free ..   ..   Cc **7**
Woolwich Arsenal.—Tuesdays and Thursdays, 10-4, by order from Director-
General of Ordnance. Repository, daily, 10-5, *free.*

THEATRES.

Places can be secured at the Box Office of each Theatre between 10 and 5. In a few
cases a charge of 1s. is made for this accommodation.

Full Dress is no longer required in any part of the house, but ladies in Stalls or Boxes
are required to take off their bonnets. In the Opera-houses, however, full dress is *de
rigueur*, except in the Amphitheatre (Upper Boxes) and Gallery. See daily papers for
full particulars. The principal Theatres are :—

Adelphi, 411 Strand ..   ..   ..   Cb **7**
Avenue, Northumberland Avenue Cb **7**
Britannia, 117 Hoxton St., in the
north - east of London (chiefly
melodrama, farce, and panto-
mime) ..   ..   Bc **9**
Comedy, Panton Street, Haymarket Cb **7**
Court, corner of Sloane Sq., Chelsea Ba **12**
Covent Garden (Royal Italian
Opera), Bow Street ..   ..   Cb **7**
Criterion, Piccadilly Circus ..   Bb **7**
Daly's, Leicester Square ..   ..   Cb **7**
Drury Lane, Catherine St., Strand Db **7**
Elephant and Castle, New Kent Rd Bb **13**
Gaiety, 345 Strand ..   ..   ..   Db **7**
Garrick, Charing Cross Road ..   Cb **7**
Globe, Newcastle Street, Strand ..   Db **7**
Grand, High Street, Islington ..   Ac **9**
Haymarket, Haymarket ..   ..   Cb **7**
Hengler's Circus, 7 Argyll Street,
Regent Street ..   ..   ..   Bc **8**
Imperial (Aquarium), Tothill Street Cc **7**
Lyceum, Wellington Street, Strand Db **7**

Lyric, Shaftesbury Avenue..   ..   Bb **7**
Metropole, Camberwell ..   ..   Cc **13**
Opera Comique, 209 Strand..   ..   Db **7**
Parkhurst, Holloway ..   ..   Db **10**
Prince of Wales, Coventry Street,
Leicester Square ..   ..   ..   Cb **7**
Prince of Wales, Greenwich ..
Princess, 150 Oxford Street ..   Bc **8**
Queen's, Lavender Hill, S.W. ..   Cc **12**
Royalty, 73 Dean Street, Soho ..   Ba **7**
St. James's, King Street ..   ..   Bc **7**
Savoy, Beaufort Buildings, Strand Db **7**
Shaftesbury, Shaftesbury Avenue Cb **7**
Standard, 204 High St., Shoreditch Ca **6**
Strand, 168 Strand ..   ..   ..   Db **7**
Stratford, High Street, Stratford Cb **14**
Surrey, 124 Blackfriars Road ..   Ed **7**
Terry's, 105 Strand ..   ..   ..   Db **7**
Trafalgar, St. Martin's Lane ..   Cb **7**

Vaudeville, 404 Strand ..   ..   Cb **7**
West London, 69 Church St., W. Db **11**

MUSIC HALLS.

Alhambra, Leicester Square	Cb 7	London Pavilion, Piccadilly Circus	Bb 7
Bedford, High St., Camden Town, N.W.	Cc 10	Metropolitan, 267 Edgware Road	Cb 11
		Middlesex, Drury Lane	Db 17
Cambridge, Commercial Street, Bishopsgate, E.C.	Da 6	New Olympic, Wych Street. Strand	Db 7
		New Pavilion, Mile End Road	Bb 14
Canterbury, Westminster Bridge Road, S.E.	Dd 7	Oxford, Oxford Street	Ca 8
		Palace, Shaftesbury Avenue	Cb 7
Collins's, Islington Green, N.	Ac 9	Paragon of Varieties, Mile End Rd.	Bb 14
Eastern Empire, Bow Road	Cb 14	Queen's, Poplar	Cb 14
Eden, Little Queen Street	Dc 8	Royal, 242 High Holborn	Dc 8
Empire, Leicester Square	Cb 7	Sadler s Wells, Rosebery Avenue	Ea 8
Forrester's, Cambridge Road, East	Cc 9	South London, London Road, S.E.	Bb 13
Gatti's, Westminster Bridge Road	Cb 7	Standard, Victoria Street	Bd 7
Gatti's, Villiers Street, Strand	Db 7	Tivoli Theatre of Varieties, Strand	Cb 7
Hoxton, Hoxton Street, N.	Bc 9	Trocadero, Shaftesbury Avenue	Cb 7
London, Shoreditch	Ca 4	Variety, 20 Pitfield Street, Hoxton	Bd 9

ENTERTAINMENTS AND CONCERTS.

Agricultural Hall, Islington, N.—Mohawk Minstrels. and Cattle, Horse, and other Shows .. Ac 9

Albert Hall, South Kensington—Has a splendid organ .. Cc 11

Alexandra Palace, Muswell Hill.—Open 10 a.m. to 9 p.m. Admission. 1s. Bands at 1, 3, and 6. Concerts at 4 and 7.30. Circus, &c. (*See* daily papers.) It is reached by rail from Broad Street (City), Moorgate Street, or King's Cross..

Aquarium, Royal, near Westminster Abbey.—Admission 1s. .. Cc 7

Botanic Gardens, Regent's Park.—Admission by orders from Fellows .. Ab 8

Crystal Palace, Sydenham. Open 10 a.m. to 8 p.m. Admission, 1s. Concert at 12.30 and 4.30. Organ at 6. Circus, Fireworks, Aquarium, &c. (*See* daily papers.) Accessible by rail from Victoria, London Bridge, or Ludgate Hill ..

Earl s Court, Annual Exhibition .. Ba 12

Egyptian Hall, Piccadilly.—Concerts, Exhibitions, &c. .. Bb 7

Horticultural Society's Gardens, South Kensington.—Daily, 9 to sunset. Admission, 1s. ; Mondays, 6d. Band on Saturdays, afternoon .. Cc 11

Moore and Burgess's (Christy) Minstrels, St. James's Hall, Piccadilly .. Bb 7

Niagara Hall, St. James's Park Station.—Real Ice Skating .. Ec 7

Olympia or **National Agricultural Hall**, Addison Road, Kensington.—Exhibitions, Shows, Sports, &c. .. Bc 11

People s Palace, Mile End Road ..

Tussaud's (Madame) Exhibition, Euston Road, near Baker Street.—Open, 10 to 10. In the evening. Music. Collection of Wax Figures, &c. Admission, 1s. ; Chamber of Horrors, 6d. extra .. Db 11

West Brompton and **Stamford Bridge Grounds**.—Athletic Sports, &c. ..

Zoological Gardens, Regent s Park.—Admission, 1s. ; on Mondays, 6d. ; on Sundays only by order from a member .. Aa 8

Morning Concerts generally begin at 3; Evening Concerts at 8. The principal Concert Halls are :—

St. George's Hall, Regent Street .. Eb 11

St. James's Hall, Regent Street and Piccadilly .. Bb 7

Floral Hall, next to Covent Garden Theatre .. Cb 7

Queen's Hall, Langham Place .. Ba 7

There are Concert Halls at the **Royal Aquarium**, the **Crystal Palace**, the **Alexandra Palace**, and the **Albert Palace**.

The Leading Musical Societies of London are the **Sacred Harmonic Society**, the **Philharmonic Society**, the **New Philharmonic Society**, the **National Choral Society, Carter's Choir**, and the **London Choral Union**.

PRINCIPAL HOSPITALS.

Bethlehem, Lambeth Road, S.E.	Ed 7	London, Whitechapel Road, E. ..	Eb 6
Cancer, Fulham Road, Brompton, S.W.	Ca 12	Metropolitan Free, Devonshire Square, E.	Bb 14
Charing Cross, Agar Street, Strand, W.C.	Cb 7	Middlesex, Mortimer St., Berners Street, W.	Bc 8
Chelsea Hospital, Chelsea	Db 12	Ophthalmic, 19 King William Street, W.C.	Cb 7
Consumption, Fulham Road, Brompton, S.W.	Ca 12	Orthopædic, 297 Oxford Street, W.	Bc 8
Dental, Leicester Square	Cb 7	Poplar, 9 Barking Road, E.	
Fever, Liverpool Rd., Islington, N.	Ac 9	Royal Free, Gray's Inn Rd., W.C.	Db 8
Foundling, Guildford Street, Mondays, 10-4; Sundays, 11-3. Visitors, on leaving after the Sunday service, are expected to place a donation upon the plate ..	Db 8	Sick Children, Great Ormond Street, W.C.	Db 8
		St Bartholomew's, Smithfield, E.C.	Ab 6
		St George's, Hyde Park Corner, W.	Ac 7
French, 10 Leicester Place, W.C. ..	Cb 7	St Luke's, Old St., City Road, E.C.	Bd 9
German, Dalston Lane, E.	Cb 9	St Mary's, Cambridge Place, Paddington, W.	Cb 11
Great Northern, Holloway Rd., N.		St Thomas', on Albert Embankment, opposite Houses of Parliament	Dc 7
Greenwich Hospital			
Guy's, St Thomas Street, Borough, S.E.	Bd 6		
Homœopathic, Great Ormond Street, W.C.	Db 8	University College, Gower Street, W.C.	Bb 8
King's College, Portugal Street, Lincoln's Inn Fields, W.C. ..	Da 7	West London, Hammersmith Road Westminster, Broad Sanctuary, S.W.	Cc 7

MARKETS.

Bermondsey Market, for hides and leather.—Bermondsey, S.E.	Ca 13
Billingsgate, Thames Street, is the wholesale fish market of London	Cc 6
Borough Market, Southwark.—Fruit and vegetables	Bb 13
Columbia Market, for the sale of fish.—Bethnal Green	Cd 9
Covent Garden, for the sale of vegetables, fruit, and flowers. Market days,— Tuesday, Thursday, and Saturday; but fruit and flowers are on sale every day ..	Cb 7
Cumberland Market, Regent's Park, for the sale of hay	Ba 8
Foreign Cattle Market, Deptford	Cd 14
Leadenhall Market, Leadenhall Street, for meat, poultry, and game	Cc 6
Metropolitan Cattle Market, Copenhagen Fields,—Principal days, Mondays and Thursdays	Cb 10
Metropolitan Meat, Poultry, and Fish, and Fruit and Vegetable Market, Smithfield	Ab 6
Shadwell, for the sale of fish.—Shadwell, E.	Ac 14
Smithfield Hay Market, Smithfield	Ab 6
South London Fish Market, New Kent Road.—Opened in 1883.	

DINING ROOMS, &c.

Pall Mall Restaurant, 14 Regent Street (excellent dinner for 5s.).—St. James's Restaurant, 69 Regent Street (dinner, 2s. 6d. to 10s. 6d.).—Grand Café Royal, 68 Regent Street (à la carte).—Criterion, Piccadilly Circus (grill).—Burlington, New Burlington Street.—Verrey's, Regent Street.

Simpson's, 103 Strand (off joint, 2s. 6d.).—Tivoli Restaurant, 69 Strand (à la carte, grill and superior wines; music, 6-10).—Gaiety Restaurant, 343 Strand (dinner, 3s. 6d.).— Duval's, Fleet Street, opposite the Royal Courts of Justice (dinner, 3s. 6d.).—The London, 191 Fleet Street (dinner from 2s.).—Lake's, 49 Cheapside.—Pimm's, 3 Poultry.— Pursell's, 78 Cornhill, close to Royal Exchange.—Three Tuns, Billingsgate Market (fish dinners at 1 and 4, for gentlemen only).—Carr's, 265 Strand.—Gatti's, 436 Strand.—Café Monico, Regent's Quadrant.

Crosby Hall, Bishopsgate Street (dinner, 3s.); the most ancient private mansion in London.

Holborn Restaurant, 218 High Holborn (dinner, 3s. 6d.; music, 6 to 8.30 p.m.).

Stout of superior quality at the "**Horseshoe,**" corner of Tottenham Court Road and Oxford Street (Meux's).—**The Cock,** 201 Fleet Street. Ale, at Edinburgh Castle, 322 Strand. Lager Beer is sold at 395 Strand, and at nearly every one of the large Restaurants. Scotch Whisky, at "**The Edinburgh,**" Milford Lane, opposite St. Clement's Church.

Oysters, at **Scott's,** top of Haymarket; **Rule's,** 36 Maiden Lane, Strand; **Pimm's,** 3 Poultry.

CONVEYANCE AND POSTAL DIRECTORY.

Cabs.—There are two wheelers (called Hansoms, after their inventor) and four wheelers, the former being by far the more expeditious. Fares are charged either by time or distance.

Fares by distance.—1s. for first two miles, 6d. for every mile beyond, if within a radius of four miles from Charing Cross, but 1s. if cab be discharged beyond that radius.

Fares by Time.—Hansoms, 2s. 6d.; four-wheelers, 2s. for first hour; 8d. for hansoms, and 6d. for four-wheelers for every quarter of an hour beyond that time. If a driver is required to drive at a rate exceeding four miles an hour, he is entitled to 3s. or 3s. 6d. an hour. For every person beyond two, an extra charge of 6d. is made.

Flies can be hired at numerous livery stables, the usual charge for a one-horse carriage being 5s. for the first hour, and 3s. 6d. for every hour beyond. A charge of 12s. 6d. is made for taking a party to the theatre and back; 15s. to 17s. 6d. to a "party" or conversazione. The gratuity to the coachman is optional.

Railways.—These are plainly indicated upon the map. Trains run along all the Metropolitan lines at frequent intervals, and they afford the most expeditious mode of travelling, though a sightseer would no doubt give the preference to a tram-car or omnibus.

Steamers ply on the Thames above and below London Bridge. The piers, or landing stages, are shown upon the map.

Local Boats, between Chelsea and London Bridge, start every ten minutes.

Woolwich and Greenwich Boats, every half-hour, from Westminster Bridge, Charing Cross, and London Bridge.

Gravesend, at 9, 10, 10.30, and 11.30, from Westminster (during summer only).

Kew, every half-hour, beginning at 11 a.m., from London Bridge, stopping at Charing Cross, Chelsea, &c.

Boats likewise proceed to *Richmond, Hampton Court, Windsor* (from Richmond), *Margate* and *Ramsgate, Southend, Sheerness,* and *Clacton-on-Sea.*

Tramways.—They are shown upon the map, and certainly deserve the preference to Omnibuses.

Omnibuses cross London in all directions, the chief centres of traffic being Charing Cross, the extremities of Regent Street, in the West End, and the Bank, in the City. Before stepping in, ask the conductor whether the omnibus proceeds to the place you desire to reach. Pay your fare before you reach your destination. The Routes of the Omnibuses and Tramway Cars are coloured upon the Map.

Post Office.—Country letters can be posted at the General Post Office and district post offices up to 6 p.m.; at most other offices only up to 5 or 5.30 p.m. On affixing an extra halfpenny stamp they can be posted up to 7.45 p.m. at the General Post Office, up to 9 p.m. at certain railway stations, and up to 5.20 to 7 p.m. at many other offices. Letters posted before 3 a.m. are generally despatched with the early mail trains.

Commissionaires, in a dark green uniform, convey messages, &c., and can be trusted. The charge is 3d. a mile, or 6d. an hour. Office, 419 Strand.

RAILWAY TERMINI and STATIONS.

Great Western, Paddington ..	Aa 4
London and North Western, Euston Square	Ba 4
Midland, St Pancras	Ba 4
Great Northern, King's Cross ..	Ba 4
Great Eastern, Liverpool Street	Ca 4
Tilbury and Southend, Fenchurch Street	Cb 14
South Eastern, London Bridge, Cannon St., and Charing Cross	Cb 14
North London, Broad Street ..	Ca 4
Brighton and South Coast, London Bridge and Victoria ..	Cb 14
London, Chatham, and Dover, Holborn Viaduct and Victoria ..	Bb 4
Metropolitan and District Railways run round the inner circle, and have branches to Hammersmith, St John's Wood, Pinner, New Cross, &c.	Ba 4

Addison Road (Kensington) ..	Ab 4	Denmark Hill	
Aldersgate Street	Ca 4	Deptford	Ce 14
Aldgate..	Ca 4	Deptford Road	Cb 4
Aldgate East	Ba 4	Dulwich	
Baker Street	Ba 4	Earl's Court	Ab 4
Barnsbury	Cb 12	East Cheap	Cc 6
Battersea	Db 12	Edgware Road (L. & N. W.) ..	Aa 4
Battersea Bridge	Db 12	Edgware Road (Metro.) ..	Ba 4
Battersea Park	Cc 11	Elephant and Castle.. ..	Cb 4
Bayswater (Queen's Road) ..	Cb 4	EUSTON (L. & N. W.) ..	Ba 4
Bermondsey	Cb 4	Farringdon Street	Ba 4
Bermondsey, South	Cb 4	Fenchurch Street	Cb 4
Bethnal Green	Ca 4	Finchley Road (L. & N. W.) ..	Aa 4
Bishopsgate (Dis. Ry.) ..	Ca 4	Finchley Road (Midland) ..	Aa 4
Bishopsgate (Great Eastern) ..	Ca 4	Finchley Road (Metro.) ..	
Bishop's Road	Aa 4	Finsbury Park..	
Blackfriars Bridge	Bb 4	Fulham	
Blackheath	5	Globe Road	Ca 4
Blackheath Hill	16	Gloucester Road	Ab 4
Blackwall	Dc 14	Gospel Oak	Bb 10
Borough Road	Bb 4	Gower Street	Ba 4
Bow		Greenwich	Ce 14
Bow Road	Cb 14	Grosvenor Road	Bb 4
Bricklayers' Arms	Cb 4	Hackney	Ca 4
Brixton	15	Hackney Downs	
BROAD STREET	Ca 4	Haggerston	Ca 4
Brockley		Hammersmith	Aa 12
Bromley-by-Bow	Cb 14	Hampstead	Ab 10
Brompton	Ab 4	Hampstead Heath	Bb 10
Brondesbury	Aa 4	Hatcham	Cb 4
Burdett Road	15	Haverstock Hill	Bb 10
Camberwell New Road ..		Herne Hill	
Cambridge Heath	Ca 4	Highbury (Islington) ..	Ba 4
Camden (Chalk Farm) ..	Ba 4	Highgate Road	Cb 10
Camden Road..	Ba 4	HOLBORN VIADUCT ..	Ba 4
Camden Town	Ba 4	Holloway	
CANNON STREET (S.E.) ..	Cb 4	Homerton	Db 9
Canning Town	5	Honor Oak	
Canonbury	Ca 4	Hornsey Road	
Cannon Street (Metro.) ..		Islington (Highbury) ..	Ba 4
Catford Bridge		Junction Road..	Ca 10
Chalk Farm, Camden ..	Ba 4	Kensal Green	Aa 4
CHARING CROSS (S.E.) ..	Bb 4	Kensington (Addison Road) ..	Ab 4
Charing Cross (Metro.) ..		Kensington (High Street) ..	Ab 4
Chelsea	Ab 4	Kensington West	Ab 4
Clapham	15	Kentish Town	Ba 4
Clapham Junction	15	Kilburn	Aa 4
Clapton	5	KING'S CROSS (G. N.) ..	Ba 4
Coborn Road	Ba 14	King's Cross (Metro.) ..	Ba 4
Crouch End		Ladbroke Grove Rd. (Notting Hill)	Aa 4
Crouch Hill		Ladywell	5
Crystal Palace..		Latimer Road..	Aa 4
Custom House	5	Leman Street	Cb 4
Dalston Junction	Ca 4	Lewisham Junction	

Lewisham Road	..	..	..		16
Limehouse	..	..	..	Dc	14
LIVERPOOL STREET	..	..	Ca	4
LONDON BRIDGE	..	..	..	Cb	4
London Fields	..	..	..	Ca	4
Lordship Lane	..	..	..		
Loudoun Road	..	..	..	Aa	4
Loughborough Junction	..	..			
Loughborough Park	..	..			
Low Leyton	..	..	..		16
Ludgate Hill	..	..	.	Bb	4
Maida Vale (Kilburn)	..	..	Aa	4
Mansion House	..	..	Cb	4
Mark Lane	..	..	..	Cb	4
Marlborough Road	..	..	Aa	4
Maze Hill (Greenwich)	..	..	De	14
Mildmay Park	..	..	..	Ca	4
Mile End	..	..	..	Ca	4
Millwall Docks	..	..	..	Cd	14
Millwall Junction	..	..	..	Cc	14
Monument	..	..	..	Cb	4
Moorgate Street	..	..	..	Ca	4
New Cross	..	..	..	Be	14
Nine Elms	..	..	..	Bb	4
Notting Hill (Ladbroke Grove Rd.)		Aa	4
Notting Hill Gate	..	..	..	Ab	4
Nunhead	..	..	..	..	15
Old Ford	..	..	..	Ec	9
Old Kent Road	..	..	..	Cb	4
PADDINGTON (G. W.)	..	..	Aa	4
Parsons' Green	..	..	..	Bb	12
Peckham Rye	..	..	..		15
Poplar	..	..	..	..	Cc	14
Poplar (E. India Road)	..	..	Cc	14
Portland Road	..	..	..	Ba	4
Praed Street (Paddington)	..	..	Aa	4
Putney	..	..	..	..	
Putney Bridge	..	..	..	Bc	12
Queen's Park (W. Kil.)	..	..	Aa	4
Queen's Road (Peckham)	..		15
Queen's Road (Bayswater)	..	Cc	11
Queen's Pri. Station, N. Elms	..	Bb	4
Rectory Road	..	..	..	Ca	9
Rotherhithe	..	..	..	Cb	4
Royal Oak	..	..	..	Aa	4
St James's Park	..	..	..	Bb	4
St John's	..	..	..	..	
St John's Wood Road	..	..	Aa	4
St Mary's, Whitechapel	..	..	Ca	4
ST PANCRAS (Midland)	..	..	Ba	4
St Paul's	..	..	..	..	
Shadwell	..	..	..	..	Cb	4
Shaftesbury Road	..	..	..	
Shepherd's Bush	..	..	..	
Shoreditch (N. London)	..	..	Ca	4
Shoreditch (E. London)	..	..	Eb	6
Sloane Square	..	..	..	Bb	4
Snow Hill	..	..	..	Ba	4
South Kensington	..	..	Ab	4
Spa Road (Bermondsey)	..	Cb	4
Stamford Hill	..	..	..		5
Stepney	..	..	..		Bc	9
Stockwell N. (Clapham)	..	..	15
Stockwell S. (Brixton)	..	..	13
Stoke Newington	..	..		5
Stratford	..	..	..	..	16
Swiss Cottage	..	..	..	Aa	4
Temple	..	..	..	..	Bb	4
Tidal Basin (Victoria Docks)	..		5
Upper Holloway	..	..	..	Ca	10
Uxbridge Road	..	..	..	Ab	4
Vauxhall	..	..	..	..	Bb	4
VICTORIA	..	..	..	Bb	4
Victoria (Dis. Ry.)	..	..		
Victoria Park	..	..	..	Db	9
Walham Green	..	..	..	Ab	4
Walworth Road	..	..	..	Bb	4
Wandsworth	..	..	..	Ec	12
Wandsworth Road	..	..	..	Ec	12
Wapping	..	..	..	Cb	4
WATERLOO (S. Western)	..	..	Bb	4
Waterloo Junction	..	..	..	Bb	4
Westbourne Park	..	..	..	Aa	4
West Brompton	..	..	..	Ab	4
West End	..	..	..	..	Ab	10
West India Docks	..	..	..	Cc	14
West Kensington	..	..	..	Ba	12
Westminster Bridge	..	..	Bb	4
Whitechapel	..	..	..	Ca	4
Willesden Junction	..	..	..		5
Willow Walk	..	..	..	Cb	4
Wimbledon	..	..	..		5
Wormwood Scrubs	..	..		
York Road (Battersea)	..	..	Db	12
York Road (King's Cross)	..	..	Ba	4

PRINCIPAL LONDON CLUBS.

Albemarle	.. ..	13 Albemarle-st.
Alexandra	.. ..	12 Grosvenor-st., W.
Alpine	.. ..	8 St Martin's-pl.
Army and Navy	..	36 Pall Mall
Arthur's	.. ..	69 St James's-st.
Arts	.. ..	17 Hanover-sq
Arundel	.. ..	1 Adelphi-ter., W.C.
Athenæum	..	107 Pall Mall
Bachelors'	.. ..	8 Hamilton-pl., W.
Badminton	..	100 Piccadilly, W.
Beaufort	.. ..	32 Dover-st., W.
Boodle's	.. ..	28 St James's-st.
Brooks's	.. ..	59 St James's-st.
Burlington F. Arts	17 Savile-row
Cambridge	.. ..	76 Pall Mall
Camera	.. ..	Charing Cross-rd.
Carlton	.. ..	94 Pall Mall
Cavalry	.. ..	127 Piccadilly
Cercle de Luxe	..	68 Piccadilly
Cigar Club	.. ..	6 Waterloo-pl., S.W.
City Carlton	..	St Swithin's-lane
City Conservative		Lombard-st.
City Liberal	..	Walbrook
City of London	..	19 Old Broad-st., E.C.
Cobden	.. ..	Has no Club House
Cocoa Tree	..	64 St James's-st.
Conservative	..	74 St James's-st.
Constitutional	..	Northumberl'd-av.

Crichton	10	Adelphi-ter.
Devonshire ..	50	St James's-st.
E. India United Ser.	16	St James's-sq.
Eldon	27	Chancery-lane
Farmers'		Salisbury-sq. Hotel
Garrick	15	Garrick-st., Cov.gd.
German Athenæum	93	Mortimer-st., W.
Grafton	10	Grafton-st., W.
Green Room ..	20	Bedford-st., W.C.
Gresham	1	Gresham-pl., E.C.
Grosvenor	135	New Bond-st., W.
Guards'	70	Pall Mall
Gun Club		Wood-la., Not'g-hl.
Hogarth	36	Dover-st., W.
Hurlingham ..		Fulham, S.W.
Hyde Park ..		Piccadilly
Isthmian	150	Piccadilly
Junior Army&Navy	10	St James's-st.
Junior Athenæum	116	Piccadilly
Junior Carlton ..	30 to 35	Pall Mall
Junior Conservative	43	Albemarle-st.
Junr. Constitutional		Piccadilly
Junior United Ser.		Charles-st..St Ja's's
Kennel	6	Cleveland-row
Lancaster		Savoy, W.C.
Law Society ..	103	Chancery-lane
Lords (M.C.C.) ..		St John's Wd. Rd.
Marlborough ..	52	Pall Mall, S.W.
National	1	Whitehall-gardens
Nat. Conservative	9	Pall Mall
Nat. Liberal ..		Whitehall-pl.,S.W.
Naval and Military	94	Piccadilly
New Club	4	Grafton-st.
New Oxf. and Cam.	20	Albemarle-st.
New Salisbury ..		St James-sq.
New University ..	57	St James s-st.
Oriental	18	Hanover-sq., W.
Orleans	29	King-st.,St James's
Oxford and Cambridge	71	Pall Mall
Pall Mall	7	Waterloo-pl., W.
Playgoers'		Gatti's, Adelphi
Portland	9	St James's-sq.
Press	7	Wine Office-court, Fleet-st.
Primrose	5	Park-pl.,St James's
Prince's Racquet ..		Knightsbridge
Raleigh	16	Regent-st., S.W.
Reform	104	Pall Mall, S.W.
Royal Canoe ..	11	Buck'gh m-st.W.C.
Royal Societies' ..		St James's
Royal Water Colour Society of Arts ..	5a	Pall Mall East
Russell Whist ..	55	Gt.Coram-st.,W.C.
St George's ..	4	Hanover-sq., W.
St George's Chess	87	St James's-st.
St James's	106	Piccadilly
St Stephen's ..	1	Bridge-st., Westm.
Savage	6	Adelphi-ter.
Savile	107	Piccadilly, W.
Scottish	39	Dover-st. W.
Smithfield Cattle ..	12	Hanover-sq.
Thatched House..	86	St James's-st.
Travellers'	106	Pall Mall
Turf	85	Piccadilly
Union		Trafalgar-sq.
United Service ..	116	Pall Mall
United University	1	Suffolk-st.
Univer. for Ladies	31	New Bond-st.
Victoria	18	Wellington-st.W.C.
Wellington ..	1	Grosvenor-pl.
Whitehall	47	Parliament-st.
White's	37	St James's-st.
Windham	13	St James's-sq.
Yorick	6	Beaufort Buildings, W.C.

ENVIRONS OF LONDON.

Suburban Resorts, &c.

Abbey Wood, 11¼ m. by *South Eastern Railway* from Charing Cross, or Cannon-street.

Acton Green, 8 m. by *District Railway* from Mansion House.

Anerley, 11¼ m. by *Brighton and South Coast Railway* from Victoria, or London Bridge.

Ashdown Forest, 39 m. by *London, Brighton, and South Coast Ry.* to Forest Row Stn.

Ashford, 17 m. by *South Western Railway* from Waterloo Station.

Ashtead and **Ashtead Park,** near Epsom.

Barking, 7½ m. by *Great Eastern Railway* from Fenchurch-street, or *North London Ry.*

Banstead Downs (Surrey), 16 m. by *London, Brighton, and South Coast Railway.*

Barnes (Surrey), 7 m. by *South Western Railway* from Waterloo, or from Ludgate Hill.

Barnet, 9 m. by *Great Northern Railway* from King's Cross, or Moorgate-street.

Battersea Park, by river. or *London, Chatham, and Dover Railway.*

Beaconsfield, 18¼ m. by *Great Western Railway* from Paddington to Slough.

Beckenham, 9 m. by *Chatham and Dover Railway* from Ludgate Hill, or Victoria.

Beckton, 8 m. by *Great Eastern Railway* from Liverpool-street.

Beddington, 9¼ m. by *Brighton and S. Coast R.* from Victoria, or London B.; also Waterloo.

Belmont, 13 by *Brighton and South Coast Railway* from Victoria, or London Bridge.

Belvedere, 10¼ m. by *S. E. Ry.* from Charing Cross, or Cannon-street; also London Bridge.

Bexley, 13¼ m. by *South Eastern Railway* from Charing Cross, or Cannon-street.

Bisley, 28 m. by *London and South Western Railway* from Waterloo. Annual meeting of National Rifle Association.

Boxhill, near Dorking, 25 m. by rail from London Bridge, or Victoria. Coach from Hatchett's, Piccadilly, at 10.30 a.m.

Brasted and Brasted Park (Kent), 20 m. by rail from London Bridge.

Bricket Wood (Herts), 3¼ m. from St. Albans. By rail from Euston.

Brockwell Park, by *London, Chatham, and Dover Railway* to Herne Hill.

Bromley (Kent), 12½ m. by *South Eastern Railway* from Charing Cross, or Cannon-street, London Bridge ; also *London, Chatham, and Dover Railway*.

Bromley (Middlesex), 3½ m. by *Tilbury & Southend R.* from Fenchurch-st., or *N. Lond. R.*

Broxbourn and Broxbournbury Park (Herts), by rail from Liverpool-st.), and St. Pancras.

Buckhurst Hill, 10 m. by *Great Eastern Railway* from Liverpool-st. and Fenchurch-st.

Burnham Beeches, by omnibus daily from Slough Station. Through tickets by *Great Western Railway*. **Stoke Pogis** Church, scene of Gray's *Elegy*, is near Slough.

Carshalton (Surrey), 13 m. by *Lond., Brighton, & South Coast Ry.* from London Bridge.

Catford Bridge, 7¼ m. by *S. E. Ry.* from Charing Cross, Cannon-street, or London Bridge.

Chadwell Heath, 9¼ m. by *Great Eastern Railway* from Liverpool-street.

Cheam (Surrey), 13 m. by *L., B., and S. C. Ry.* from London Bridge, or Victoria.

Cheshunt (Herts), 17 m. by *Great Eastern Railway*. Cheshunt Great House and Cromwell Relics, also **Temple Bar** re-erected at entrance to Theobald's Park.

Chigwell-lane, 12 m. by *Great Eastern Railway* from Liverpool-street, and Fenchurch-st.

Chingford and Epping Forest, 12 m. by *Great Eastern Ry.* from Liverpool-street.

Chislehurst (Kent), 11 m. by *South Eastern Railway* from London Bridge, or by *London, C., and Brighton Railway* to Bickley Station, thence on foot.

Chiswick, 8¼ m. by *South Western Ry.* from Waterloo, or from Ludgate Hill Station.

Clapham Common, by tramway car from Blackfriars or Westminster Bridge.

Cobham (Surrey), 18 m. by *South Western Railway* from Waterloo.

Croydon, 12 m. by *S. Eastern Ry.* from Charing Cross, also London Bridge, or Victoria.

Dagenham, 11½ m. by *Great Eastern Railway* from Fenchurch-street.

Dartford, 11¼ m. by *South Eastern Railway* from Charing Cross, or Cannon-street.

Denmark Hill, 4 m. by *Chat. & Dov. Ry.* from Victoria, or Ludgate Hill; also London B.

Epsom and Epsom Downs, by rail from London Bridge and Victoria.

Farthing Down, 15 m. by *South Eastern Railway* to Coulsdon Station, nearest point.

Forty Hill, Enfield, 10 m. by *Great Northern Railway* from King's Cross.

Gipsy Hill, 7¼ m. by *Brighton and South Coast Ry.* from Victoria, or London Bridge.

Gravesend, 30 m. by steamboat daily from London Bridge ; also by rail.

Greenwich, by tram-car from Blackfriars, steamboat, or *South Eastern Railway*, 5 m. Royal Naval College, Greenwich Hospital, Painted Hall and Chapel, daily, 10-7 and 10-3; Saturdays, after 1 p.m. Hall also on Sundays. 1 p.m. Naval Museum, Ships' Models, &c., daily, Friday and Saturday excepted, 10-4. Observatory by permission of Astronomer-Royal.

Hampstead Heath, by rail from Broad-street, or Mansion House omnibus, passing along Tottenham Court-road ; also by tram-car. The **Vale of Health** is about half a mile from the station.

Hampton Court Palace, 15 m. by rail from Waterloo, or by steamer from London Bridge at 10 a.m., landing passengers at gates of the palace. Open daily, except Friday, free, from 10 a.m. to 6 p.m. April to October, and till 4 during winter, and the gardens till dusk. **Bushey Park** is on the opposite side of Hampton Wick Road from the palace gardens.

Hanwell, 12 m. by *District Ry.* from Mansion House ; also *N. London* or *Great Western*.

Harrow-on-the-Hill, 15 m. by rail from Mansion House or *L. and N. W. Ry.* from Euston.

Hatfield House and Park, 20 m. by *Great Northern Railway* from King's Cross. Residence of Lord Salisbury.

Hayes (Middlesex), 11 m. by *South Western Railway* from Paddington, or *District Ry.*

Hayes Common (Kent), 14 m. by *South Eastern Ry.* from Charing Cross, or Cannon-st.

Hendon, 8 m. by *Midland Railway* from Moorgate-street and St. Pancras.

Herne Hill, 5 m. by *London, Chatham, and Dover Railway* from St. Paul's, or Victoria.

High Barnet, 14 m. by *Great Northern Railway* from King's Cross.

Honor Oak, 7¼ m. by *Chatham and Dover Railway* from Victoria, or Ludgate Hill.

Hornsey, 5¼ m. by *Great Northern Railway* from Moorgate-street, or *Midland Railway*.

Hounslow Barracks, 13 m. by *District Railway* from Mansion House.

Isleworth, 12 m. by *South Western Ry.* from Waterloo, Ludgate Hill, or Broad-street.

Kew Gardens, by rail from Broad-street, Moorgate-street, Waterloo, Ludgate Hill, or Mansion House ; or by steamer to Kew Pier. Open daily from 12 till dusk, and 10 on Bank Holidays.

Kingston-on-Thames, 12 m. by *South Western Railway* from Waterloo, or by water.

Knockholt Beeches, about 3 m. from Halstead Station, *South Eastern Railway*.

Ladywell, 6¼ m. by *South Eastern Railway* from Charing Cross, or Cannon-street.

Lee, 7¼ m. by *South Eastern Railway* from Charing Cross, or Cannon-street.

Leith Hill (Surrey), 5 m. from Dorking. *London, Brighton, and South Coast Railway.* Fourteen counties visible from the Tower.

Limpsfield (Surrey), by *L., B., and S. C. Ry.* to Oxted Station, 20 m. Golf links and cricket ground.

Maidenhead (Berks) 26 m. by *Great Western Railway* from Paddington.

Mitcham Common, by *South Western Railway* from Waterloo, about 8 m.

Mill Hill (Middlesex), 6 m. by *Great Northern Railway* from King's Cross.

Mortlake, 8¼ m. by rail from Waterloo, or Ludgate Hill; or by water to Barnes Pier.

Orpington and The Crays, 15 m. by *S. E. Ry.* from Charing Cross, or Cannon-street.

Ottershaw Park (Surrey), by *South Western Railway* from Waterloo to Addleston Station. The park is 2 m. from the station.

Oxshott Heath, 14 m. by *South Western Railway* from Waterloo Station.

Panshanger Park (Herts), near Cole Green Station, *Great Northern Railway,* 28 m.

Petersham Park (Surrey), near Richmond.

Pinner (Middlesex), 14 m. by *Metropolitan Railway.*

Purfleet (Essex), 15 m. by *Tilbury and Southend Railway* from Fenchurch-street. Botany Bay Gardens.

Putney (Surrey), 5 m. by rail from Waterloo; also by steamboat. Starting-point of Oxford and Cambridge annual boat-race. Putney Heath, Roehampton, and Barnes Common near.

Radlett (Herts), about 15 m. by *Midland Railway* from St. Pancras. Aldenham Lodge Park near here.

Reigate (Surrey), 24 m. by *South Eastern Railway* from London Bridge.

Richmond, 10 m. by rail from Waterloo Station, Moorgate-street. Ludgate Hill, Broad-street, and Mansion House; 15 m. by water from Waterloo Bridge. Richmond Hill, with fine view, and Park of 2253 acres; also the Pen Ponds.

Riddlesdown (Surrey), 15 m. by *South Eastern Railway,* or *London, Brighton, and South Coast Railway* to Upper Warlingham Station. Favourite picnic resort.

Rosherville Gardens, nr. Gravesend, by steamer. Return fare, including admission, 1s. 6d.

Rye House (Herts), 18 m. by *Great Eastern Railway* from Liverpool-street.

St. Albans, 21 m. by *London and North Western Ry.* from Euston. Famous abbey.

St. George's Hill and Cæsar's Camp (Surrey), near Weybridge Station, about 19 m. by *South Eastern Railway* from Waterloo.

Sevenoaks, 22 m. from Charing Cross, Victoria, or Ludgate Hill. Here is Knole Park. Ightliam Mote should also be visited.

Shirley Hills (Surrey), about 2 m. from South Croydon Station, on *London, Brighton, and South Coast Railway.* Addington, seat of the Archbishop of Canterbury, near here.

Silvertown, 8 m. by *G. E. Railway* from Liverpool-street, or *North London Ry.*

Snaresbrook, 8 m. by *Great Eastern Railway* from Liverpool-street, or *N. London Ry.*

Southall, 13 m. by *District Railway* from Mansion House, or *Great Western Railway.*

Southend-on-Sea (Essex), 40 m. by *Great Eastern Railway* from Liverpool-street.

Strawberry Hill, 12½ m. by *South Western Railway* from Waterloo, or Ludgate Hill.

Streatham Common, 8 m. by rail from Victoria, or London Bridge; or 'bus from Gracechurch-street.

Sudbury, 12 m. by *North London Railway* from Broad-street, or Euston.

Surbiton, 12 m. by *South Western Railway* from Waterloo.

Sutton (Surrey), 15 m. by *L., B., and S. C. Ry.* from Victoria, or London Bridge.

Teddington, 13 m. by *S. W. Ry.* from Waterloo, also from Ludgate Hill, or by water.

Theydon Bois (Essex), 16 m. by *Great Eastern Railway* from Liverpool-street.

Tilbury, 23 m. by *Great Eastern Ry.* from Liverpool-street; also by *North London Ry.*

Tooting Bec Common, by rail from Blackfriars, or Westminster Bridge.

Twickenham, 11½ m. by *South Western Ry.* from Waterloo. Pope's Villa, &c.

Virginia Water (Surrey), 23 m. by *South Western Railway* from Waterloo Station.

Walton-on-Thames (Surrey), 17 m. by *South Western Railway* from Waterloo.

Warlingham (Upper), 15 m. from Victoria or London Bridge Stations.

Wembley Park, near Harrow, by rail from Baker-street. Great Tower, 1150 feet high, in course of construction.

Westerham (Kent), 21 m. by *South Eastern Railway* from Charing Cross, or Cannon-st.

Wimbledon Common and Park (Surrey), 8 m. from Waterloo, Ludgate Hill, London Bridge, and Victoria.

Winchmore Hill (Middlesex), about 8 m. by rail from King's Cross, *Great Northern Ry.*

Windsor (Berks), 22 m. from Paddington or Waterloo Stn. Admission to the Castle during Queen's absence only: Mon., Tues., and Thurs., by tickets obtainable in the town.

Woolwich, by rail same as for Greenwich, and by steamer.

Plate 1

BIRD'S-EYE VIEW MAP OF CENTRAL LONDON.

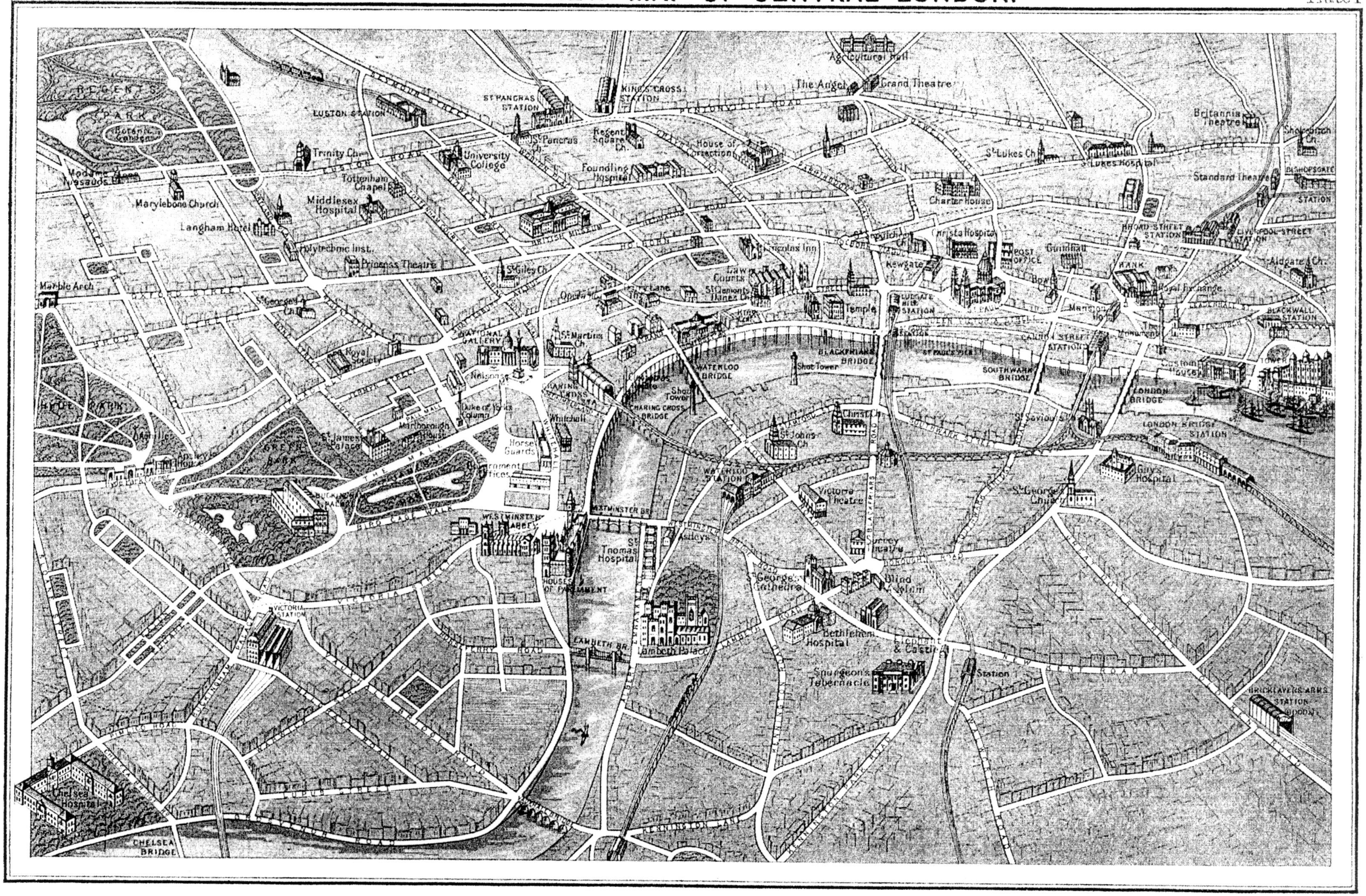

Plate 2.

LONDON COUNTY COUNCIL AND PARLIAMENTARY DIVISIONS.

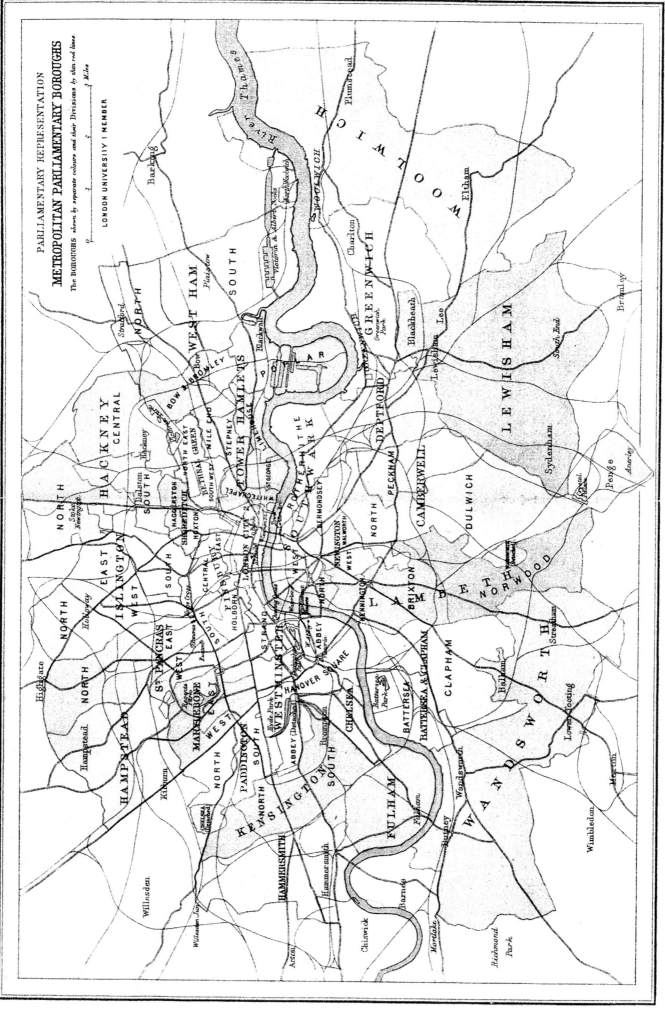

PARLIAMENTARY REPRESENTATION

METROPOLITAN PARLIAMENTARY BOROUGHS

The BOROUGHS shown by separate colours and their Divisions by thin red lines.

LONDON UNIVERSITY 1 MEMBER

Plate 3

POSTAL DISTRICTS.

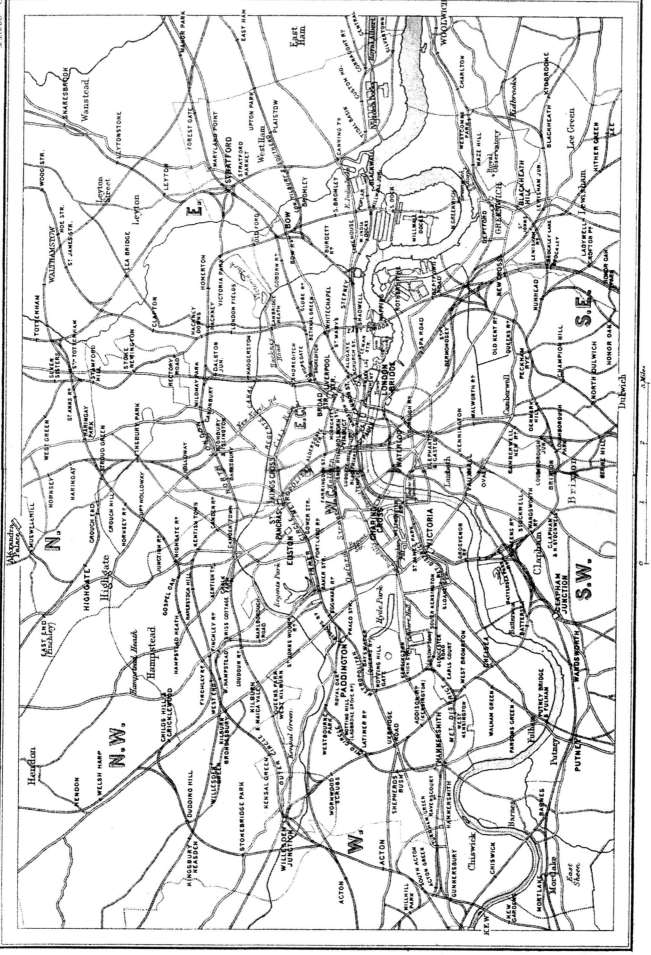

RAILWAY MAP OF CENTRAL LONDON.

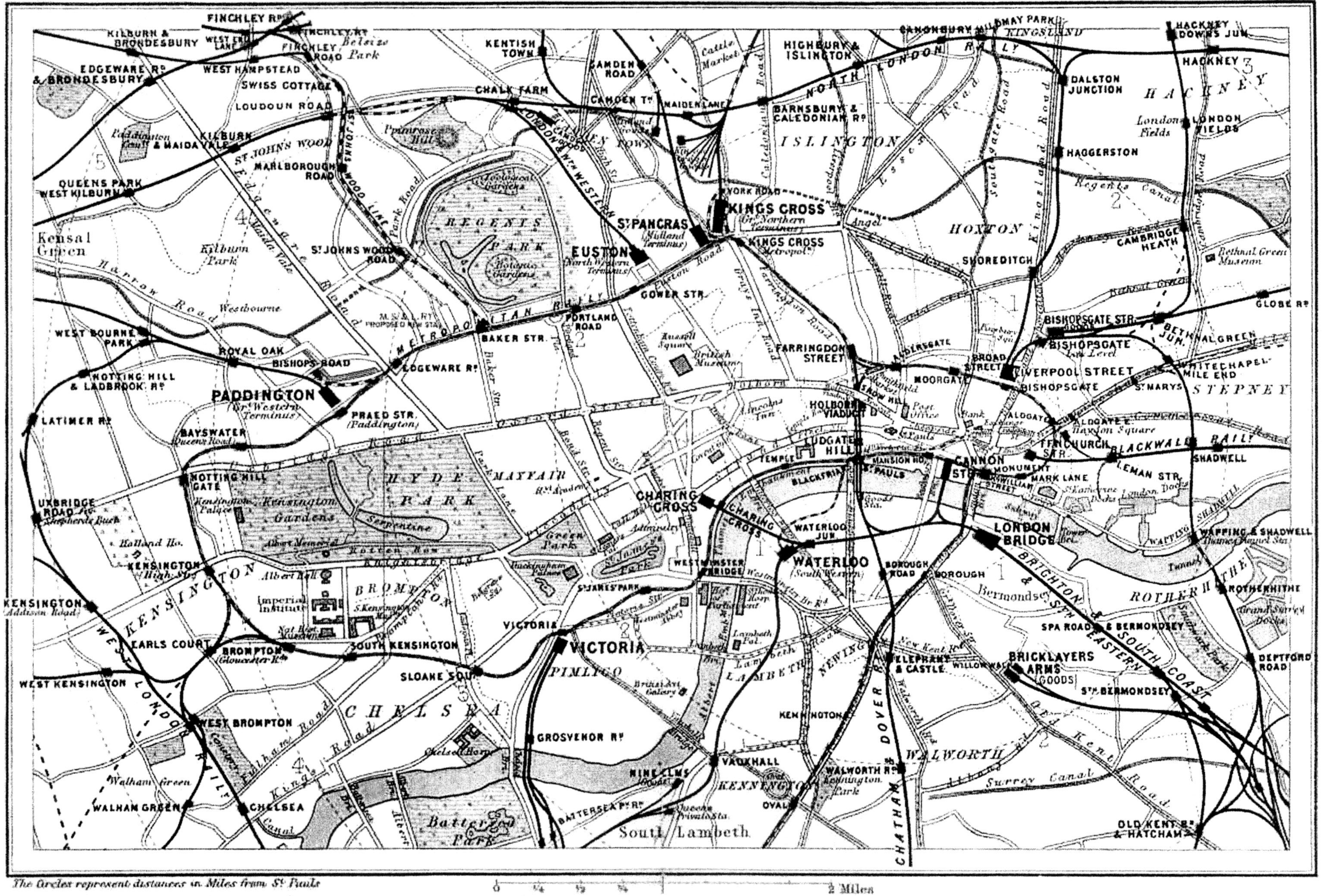

Plate 4.

The Circles represent distances in Miles from St Pauls.

2 Miles

Plate 5

RAILWAY MAP OF LONDON AND SUBURBS.

INDEX TO SECTION-MAPS IN ATLAS.

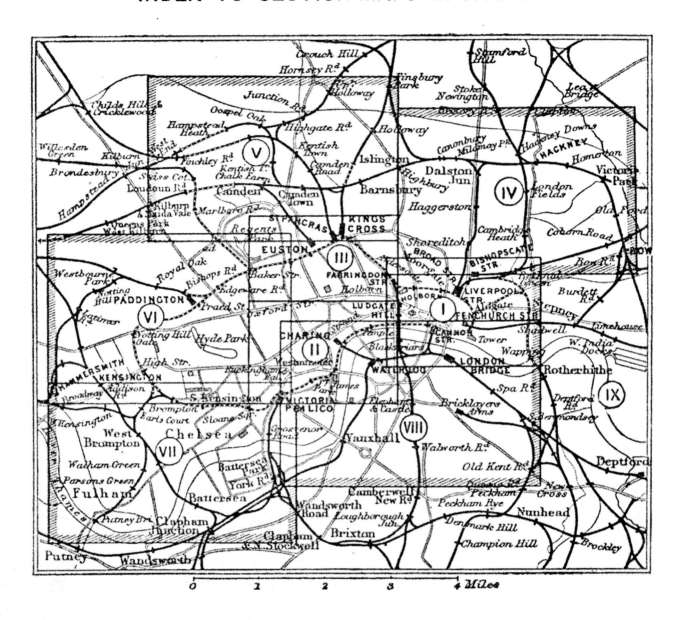

NOTE FOR CENSUS SEARCHERS

The area covered by this Atlas is roughly that of the London Census Districts;

Paddington, Kensington, Fulham, Chelsea, St George Hanover Square, Westminster, Marylebone, Hampstead, Pancras, Islington, Hackney, St Giles, Strand, Holborn, London City, Shoreditch, Bethnal Green, Whitechapel, St George in the East, Mile End Old Town, Poplar, St Saviour Southwark, St Olave Southwark, parts of Lambeth, Wandsworth, Camberwell, and Greenwich

The street index includes the major streets in each district, but not all of the minor ones.

STREET PLAN, SECTION I.

Plate 6.

Continued on Section IV

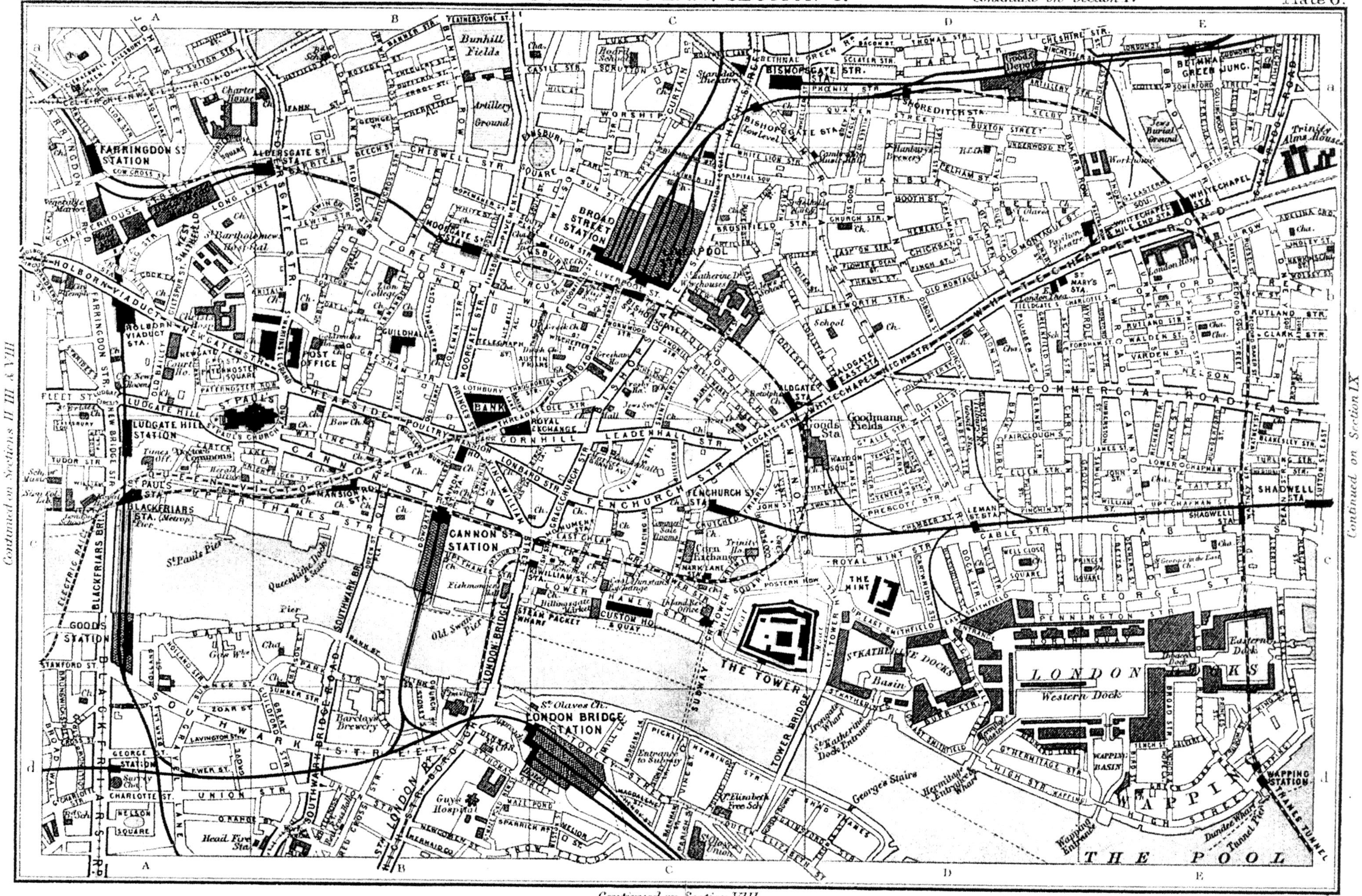

Continued on Section IX

THE POOL

THE TOWER

LONDON Western Dock

BROAD STR.

ST. KATHARINE DOCKS

THE MINT

TOWER HILL

LONDON BRIDGE STATION

CANNON ST. STATION

BANK

ROYAL EXCHANGE

BROAD STREET STATION

BISHOPSGATE

Bunhill Fields

BUNHILL ROW

WHITECHAPEL

WHITECHAPEL ROAD

COMMERCIAL ROAD

Goodmans Fields

CORNHILL

POULTRY

CHEAPSIDE

St. PAUL'S

POST OFFICE

MARTINS LE GRAND

NEWGATE ST.

LUDGATE HILL

HOLBORN VIADUCT

FARRINGDON ST. STATION

FARRINGDON STR.

NEW BRIDGE STR.

BLACKFRIARS BRIDGE

BLACKFRIARS RD.

SOUTHWARK BRIDGE RD.

GREAT GUILDFORD STR.

SOUTHWARK STR.

LONDON BRIDGE

SOUTHWARK BR.

FLEET ST.

KING WILLIAM STR.

FENCHURCH STR.

LEADENHALL STR.

HOUNDSDITCH

ALDGATE

MINORIES

ROYAL MINT STR.

CABLE STR.

CANNON STR. ROAD

NEW ROAD

ALDERSGATE STR.

MOORGATE STR.

FINSBURY

CURTAIN RD.

SHOREDITCH

BETHNAL GREEN RD.

COMMERCIAL STR.

BRICK LANE

OLD STREET

GOSWELL RD.

FARRINGDON RD.

Continued on Sections II III & VIII

Continued on Section VIII

The Plan is divided into half Mile Squares

½ Mile

STREET PLAN. *SECTION II.*

Continued on Section III

Continued on Sections VI & VII

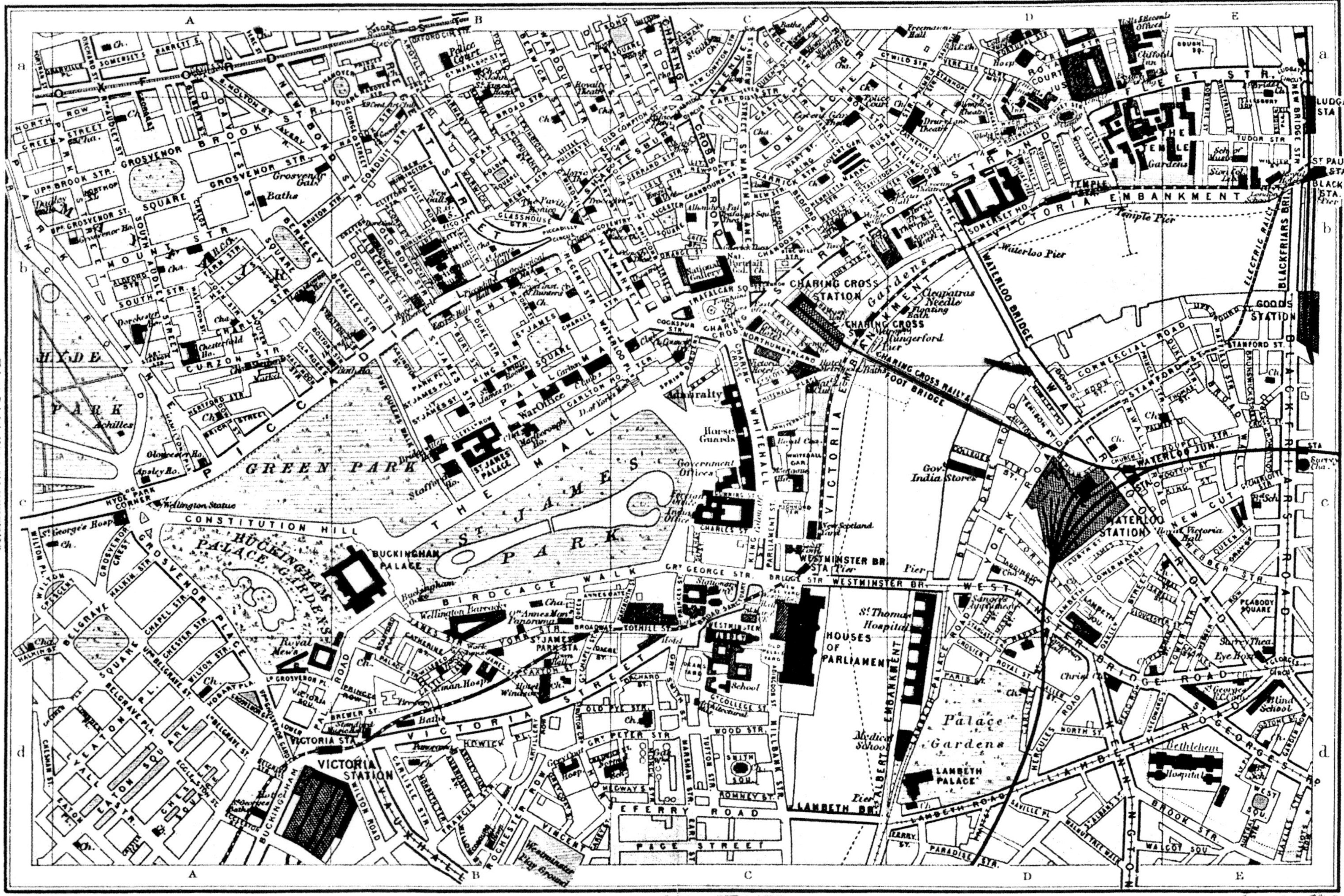

Continued on Sections J & VIII

Continued on Sections VII & VIII

0 ¼ ½ Mile

The Plan is divided into half Mile Squares

Plate 8.

STREET PLAN. SECTION III.

Continued on Section V

Continued on Sections I & IV

Continued on Section II

Continued on Sections V & II

The Plan is divided into half Mile Squares

½ Mile

ZOOLOGICAL GARDENS

REGENT'S PARK

ROYAL BOTANIC GARDENS

KING'S CROSS STATION (Northern)

ST PANCRAS STATION (Midland)

EUSTON STATION (L. & North Western)

UNIVERSITY COLLEGE

BRITISH MUSEUM

FARRINGDON ST STATION

HOLBORN VIADUCT STA.

FARRINGDON STR.

HOLBORN

EUSTON ROAD

NEW ROAD

HAMPSTEAD ROAD

TOTTENHAM COURT ROAD

PORTLAND PLACE

MARYLEBONE ROAD

HARLEY STR.

WELBECK STR.

WIGMORE STR.

BAKER STR.

PORTMAN SQUARE

MANCHESTER SQUARE

CAVENDISH SQUARE

PORTLAND ROAD

REGENT STREET

CHARING CROSS ROAD

OXFORD STREET

WARDOUR STR.

BERNERS STR.

SOHO SQUARE

BEDFORD SQUARE

RUSSELL SQUARE

TAVISTOCK SQUARE

GORDON SQUARE

TORRINGTON SQUARE

WOBURN SQUARE

BRUNSWICK SQUARE

MECKLENBURG SQUARE

BLOOMSBURY SQUARE

SOUTHAMPTON ROW

GRAY'S INN ROAD

LINCOLN'S INN

HATTON GARDEN

FETTER LANE

TEMPLE

GUILFORD STR.

DOUGHTY STR.

BEDFORD ROW

JOHN STR.

LAMB'S CONDUIT STR.

THEOBALD'S ROAD

HIGH HOLBORN

PENTONVILLE ROAD

CALEDONIAN ROAD

PENTON STR.

CLOUDESLEY RD.

LIVERPOOL ROAD

RODNEY STR.

CUMMING STR.

SOUTHAMPTON STR.

WINCHESTER STREET

WHARFDALE RD.

PANCRAS ROAD

MIDLAND GOODS DEPOT

MR. COAL DEPOT

CHALTON STREET

SEYMOUR STREET

CRESCENT

ST ANDREW'S

HIGH STR.

NEW OXFORD ST.

CHARLOTTE STR.

GREAT TITCHFIELD STR.

GREAT PORTLAND STR.

CLEVELAND STR.

ALBANY STR.

STANHOPE STR.

AUGUSTUS STR.

PARK VILLAGE EAST

PARK VILLAGE WEST

CHESTER TERRACE

CUMBERLAND YARD

REDHILL STR.

GLOUCESTER GATE

CHESTER ROAD

BROAD WALK

OSNABURGH STR.

GREAT JAMES STR.

DEVONSHIRE STR.

WEYMOUTH STR.

NEW CAVENDISH STR.

QUEEN ANNE STR.

BENTINCK STR.

GEORGE STR.

SEYMOUR STR.

ORCHARD STR.

BAKER STREET

YORK PL.

PADDINGTON STR.

MARYLEBONE STR.

DEAN STR.

POLAND STR.

ARGYLL STR.

BEAK STR.

WIMPOLE STR.

LANGHAM PL.

CARBURTON STR.

STREET PLAN. *SECTION IV.*

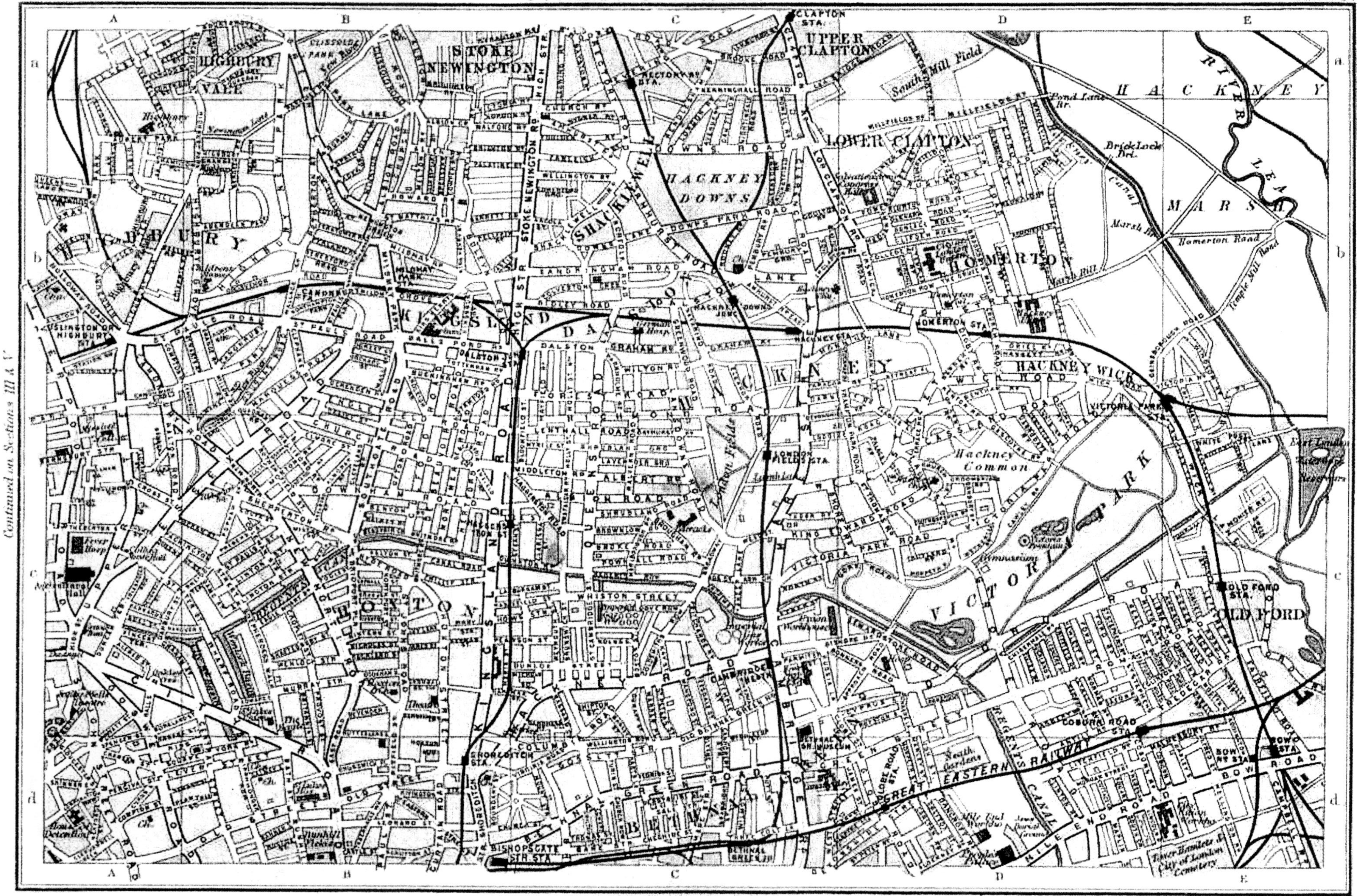
STOKE NEWINGTON
UPPER CLAPTON
LOWER CLAPTON
HACKNEY MARSH
RIVER LEA
HIGHBURY VALE
HIGHBURY
HACKNEY DOWNS
SHACKLEWELL
HOMERTON
KINGSLAND
DALSTON
HACKNEY
HACKNEY WICK
Hackney Common
VICTORIA PARK
HOXTON
OLD FORD
London Fields
REGENTS CANAL
GREAT EASTERN RAILWAY
BETHNAL GREEN
CITY ROAD
CAMBRIDGE ROAD
MILE END ROAD
BOW ROAD
CLAPTON STA.
HACKNEY STA.
HOMERTON STA.
LONDON FIELDS STA.
VICTORIA PARK STA.
OLD FORD STA.
COBURN ROAD STA.
GLOBE ROAD STA.
BOW STA.
SHOREDITCH STA.
BISHOPSGATE STA.
Continued on Sections III & V

Continued on Sections I & IX

0 ¼ ½ ¾ 1 Mile

The Plan is divided into Mile Squares

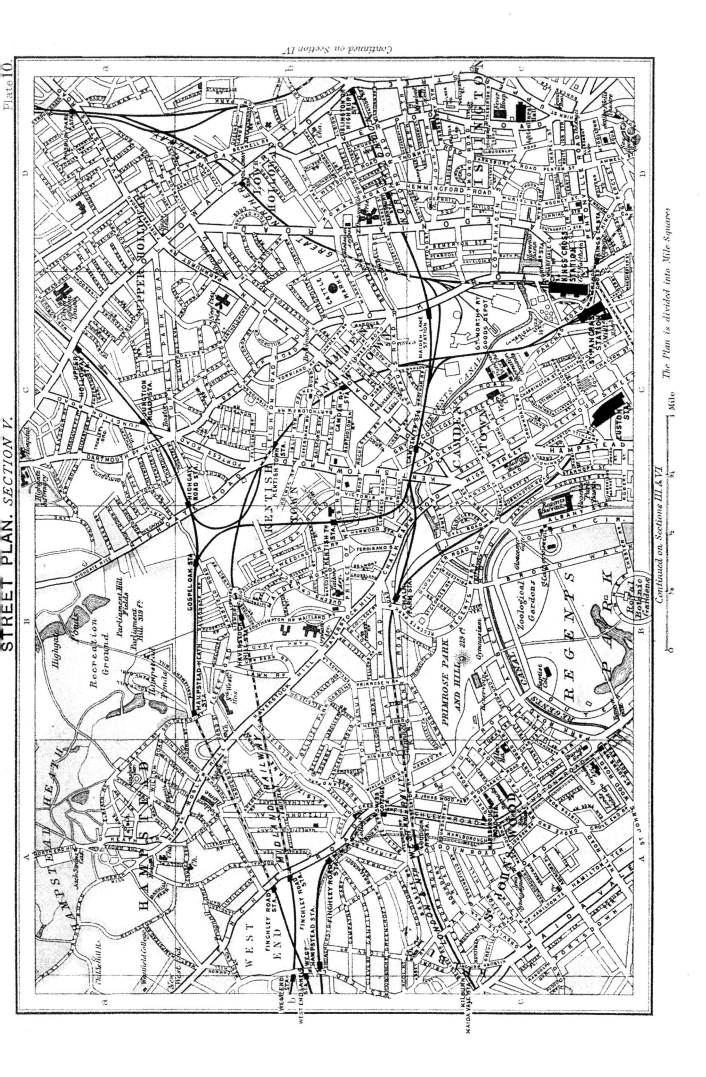

Plate 10.

STREET PLAN. SECTION V.

Continued on Section IV.

Continued on Sections III. & VI.

The Plan is divided into Mile Squares.

Plate 11.

STREET PLAN. SECTION VI.

Continued on Section V

Continued on Sections II, III & VIII

REGENT'S PARK

Royal Botanic Gardens

HYDE PARK

KENSINGTON GARDENS

GREEN PARK

BUCKINGHAM PALACE

SERPENTINE RIVER

HOLLAND PARK

WEST LONDON RAILWAY

PADDINGTON STATION

Kensal Green Cemetery

Continued on Section VII

The Plan is divided into Mile Squares

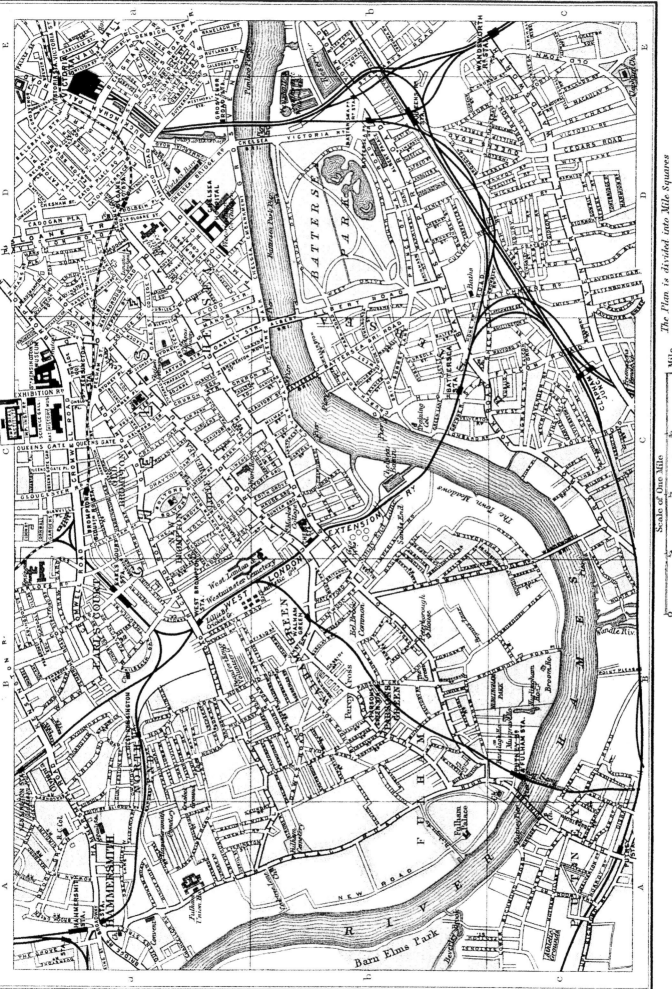

Plate 13

SOUTHWARK PARK

PECKHAM NEW TOWN

THE POOL

LONDON BRIDGE

BERMONDSEY

SOUTH WARK

BLACKFRIARS ROAD

WATERLOO STA.

KENNINGTON ROAD

WALWORTH

CAMBERWELL ROAD

CHATHAM & DOVER RY

LAMBETH

GREEN PARK

ST. JAMES'S PARK

WHITEHALL

BUCKINGHAM PALACE

LAMBETH PALACE

VAUXHALL

REGENCY STREET

British Art Gallery

Scale of One Mile

Continued on Sections I & VIII

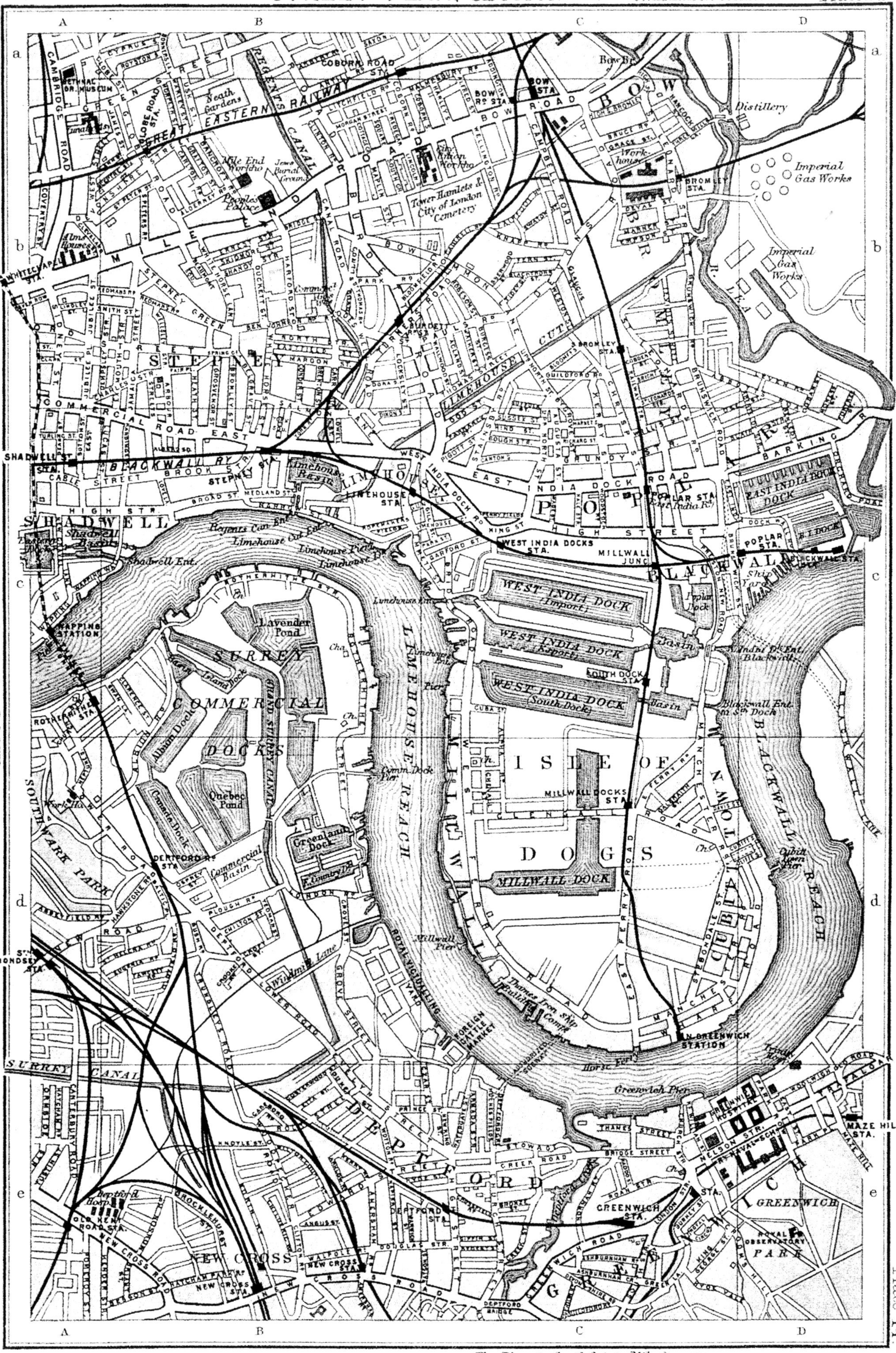

Plate 14.

The Plan is divided into Mile Squares

0 ¼ ½ ¾ 1 Mile

Plate 15.

THE THAMES TO WINDSOR.

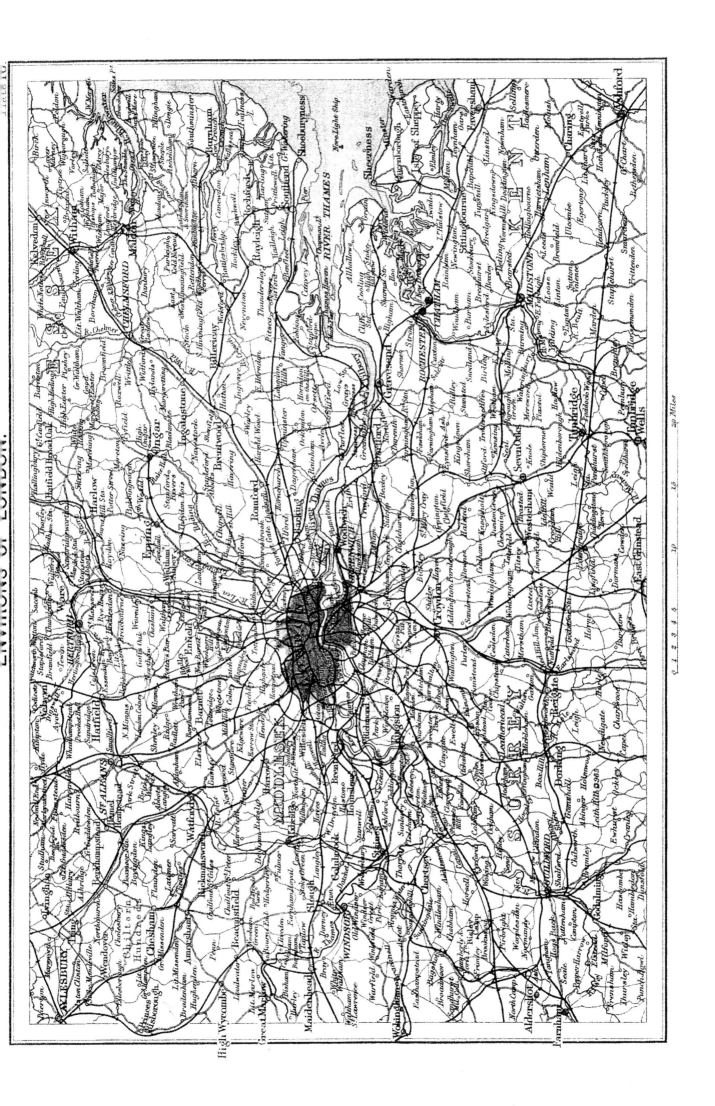

INDEX TO STREETS AND PLACES OF INTEREST.

NOTE.—The letters after the names correspond with those in the borders of the maps, and indicate the square in which the name will be found. The numbers after the letters indicate the map in the Atlas.

A-street, Kensal-green Ba 11
Abbey-pl., St John's-wd. Ac 10
  „ rd., „ „ Ac 10
  „ st., Bermondsey Cb 13
Abbott's-rd., Bromley Cb 14
Aberdeen-pk., Highby. Bb 9
Abingdon-st., Westm'r. Cd 7
Acacia-rd., StJohn's-wd. Ac10
Achilles stat., Hyde-pk. Dc 11
Acton-st., Gray's Inn-rd. Da 8
Ada-st., Hackney .. Cc 9
Adam-st., Strand .. Cb 7
Adelaide-rd. .. .. Bb 10
Adelphi Theatre, Strand Cb7
Addington-rd., Old Ford Ed9
Addison-rd., Kensington Bc11
Admiralty Off., Whitehall Cc 7
Agricultrl. Hl., Islingtn. Dc10
Alaska-st., Waterloo-rd. Dc 7
Albans-rd., Kentish-tn. Ba 10
Albany-rd., Walworth Cc 13
  „ st., Regent's-pk. Bc 8
Albemarle-st., Piccadilly Bb 7
Albert-bridge, Chelsea Cb 12
  „ embank., L'mb'h. Bb13
  „ gate, Hyde-pk. Dc 11
  „ Hall,S.Kensngtn. Cc11
  „ Memor.,Hyde-pk Cc11
  „ Palace,Battersea Db12
  „ rd., Battersea Db 12
  „ rd., Dalston .. Cc 9
  „ rd., Regent's-pk. Bc 10
  „ st., Camden-tn. Cc 10
  „ st., Islington .. Da 8
  „ st., Shadwell .. Ec 6
  „ ter., Bishop's-rd. Cb 11
  „ ter., Clapham-rd. Bc 13
Albion-dock,Roth'rhithe Bc11
  „ grove, Islington Dc 10
  „ gr., Stoke Newn. Bb 9
  „ rd., Dalston .. Cc 9
  „ rd., Hackney .. Db 9
  „ rd., Kilburn .. Ab10
  „ rd., Stoke Newn. Ba 9
  „ st., King's Cross Da 8
  „ st.,Uxbridge-rd. Db11
Aldenham-st.,Somers-tn. Ca8
Aldermanbury .. Bb 6
Alderney-rd.,Beth'l-gr. Bb 14
Aldersgate station .. Ca 4
  „ st. .. Bb 6
Aldgate station .. Ca 4
  „ st. .. .. Cc 6
  „ East station Ca 4
Aldred-rd., Walworth Bc 13

Aldrich-st.,Camden-tn. Cb 10
Alexandra-rd.,StJohn's-
  wood .. .. .. Ac 10
Alfred-pl., Tot.Court-rd. Bc 8
  „ st., City-rd. .. Ac 9
  „ st., Mile End Bb 14
  „ st., Mile End-rd. Cb 14
  „ st., Millwall .. Cc 14
Alhambra, Leicester-sq Cb 7
Alie-st.Gt.&Lit., Whtech Dc6
Allen-rd., Stoke Newn. Bb 9
  „ st., Kensington Bc 11
  „ st., Lambeth .. Dd 7
Alma-rd.,BlueA'hor-rd. Db 13
Alpha-rd., Park-rd. Db 11
Alscot-rd., Bermondsey Db 13
Amberly-rd.,Harrow-rd. Cb11
Ambrosden-av., Pimlico Bd 7
Amelia-st., Walworth-rd. Bb13
Amersham-rd.,Deptford Be14
Amherst-rd.E.,Hackney Cb9
  „ rd.,Shacklewell Cb9
Ampthill-sq.,Hmpstd-rd. Ba 8
Ampton-st.,Gray'sIn.-rd.Db8
Amwell-st., Pentonville Da 8
Andover-rd., Holloway Da 10
Andrew's-rd., Hackney Cc 9
Angel, The, Islington Ea 8
Angel-st., St Martin's-
  le-Grand .. .. Bb 6
Annette-rd. Holloway Db 10
Anthony-st.,Commer.-rd.Ec6
Appold-st., Finsbury Cb 6
Approach-rd., Vict.-pk. Dc 9
Apsley-ho.,Hy. Pk.-cor.Dc11
Arbour-st., Stepney Bb 14
Archer-st., Notting-hill Bb 11
Argyle-sq., King's Cross Ca 8
  „ st., Euston-rd. Ca 8
Argyll-pl., Regent-st. Ba 7
  „ st., Oxford-st. Ba 7
Arkwright-rd.,Hmpstd. Ab10
Arlington-st.,Camd'n-tn.Cc10
  „ New N.-rd. Bc 9
  „ Pentonville Ea 8
  „ Piccadilly Bb 7
Armagh-rd., Old Ford Ec 9
Arthur-st., Chelsea .. Ca 12
  „ Gray'sInn-rd. Db8
  „ NewOxford-st.Cc8
ArtilleryGround, City-rd. Ba6
  „ row,Victoria-st. Bd7
  „ st., Bethnal-gn. Da 6
Arundel-st., Strand .. Db 7
Ash-grove, Hackney .. Cc 9

Ashburnham-cres. and
  rd., Greenwich .. Ce 14
Ashbury-rd., Battersea Dc 12
Ashley-grove, Islington Bc 9
Ashmore-rd.,Harr'w-rd. Bb11
Asylum-rd., Peckham Dc 13
Atwood-la., Kensington Ca 12
Aubert-pk., Highbury Ab 9
Auckland-rd., Old Ford Dc 9
Audley-st. N.&S,Mayfair Ab7
Augusta-st., Poplar .. Cc 14
Augustus-st.,Rege't's-pk. Ba8
Austin Friars, Bank .. Cb 6
Ausyn-st., Lambeth .. Dc 7
Avenell-rd., Highbury Aa 9
Avenue-rd.,Camberwell Bc13
  „ rd.,Hampstead Ab10
  „ rd.,Rege't's-pk. Ac10
  „ Theatre, North-
  umberland-avenue .. Cb 7
Avery-row, Oxford-st. Ab 7
Aylesbury-st.,Clerk'nw'l. Aa6
B-street, Kensal-green Ba 11
Back Church-lane, Com-
  mercial rd. .. .. Dc 6
Back-hill, Theobald's-rd. Eb8
  „ rd., Kingsland .. Bb 9
Bacon-st., Shoreditch Da 6
Bagley-lane, Chelsea Bb 12
Baker-st., Clerkenwell Db 8
  „ Marylebone Db 11
  „ station .. Ba 4
Bakers-row,Whitechapel Eb6
Balaklava-rd. Db13
Baldwin's-gdns.,Gray's
  Inn-rd. .. .. Dc 8
BallsPond-rd.,Kingsland Bb 9
Banbury-rd., Hackney Dc 9
Bancroft-rd., Beth.-gr. Bb 14
Bank of England .. Bb 6
  „ Side, Southwark Ba 13
  „ st., Southwark Bc 6
BaptistCol'ge, Reg.'s-pk. Bc10
Barbican, Aldersgate-st. Bb 6
Barclay-st., Somers-tn. Ba 8
Barclay'sBrewery,South-
  wark .. .. .. Bd 6
Barking-rd., Poplar Dc 14
Barnsbury-rd.,Islington Dc 10
  „ st., „ Dc10
  „ station .. Ba 4
Baron-st., Pentonville Ea 8
Barrett-gr., Stoke Newn Bb 9
  „ st., Portman-sq. Aa 7
Barrow Hill-pl. .. Bc 10

Bartholomew-lane, Bank Bb **6**
  „   rd., Kent-
  ish-tn. .. .. Cb **10**
Basinghall-st. .. .. Bb **6**
Bath-st., City-rd. .. Bd **9**
  „   Columbia-rd. Cc **9**
Battersea .. .. Cb **12**
  „   Bridge .. Cb **12**
  „   Bridge-rd. .. Cb **12**
  „   Park .. Dc **12**
  „   Park-pier, Bat. Db**12**
  „   Park-rd. .. Dc **12**
Battle Bridge-rd., Pan-
  cras-rd. .. .. Ca **8**
Bayham-st., Camden-tn. Cc **10**
Baynes-row, Far'gdon-rd. Db**8**
Bayswater .. .. Cb **11**
  „   station .. Ab **4**
Beale-rd., Old Ford .. Dc **9**
Bear-lane, Southwark Ad **6**
Beaufort-st., Chelsea Cb **12**
Beaumont-sq., Mile End Bb**14**
  „   st., Marylebone Ab**8**
Bedford-pl., Bloomsbury Cc**8**
  „   row, Holborn Dc **8**
  „   sq., Bloomsbury Cc**8**
  „   sq., E. Com-
  mercial-rd. .. .. Eb **6**
Bedford-st., Ampth'l-sq. Ba **8**
  „   st., Bedford sq. Dc **8**
  „   st., Com'erc'l-rd. Eb**6**
  „   st., Strand .. Cb **7**
Beech-st., Barbican .. Bb **6**
Belgrave-pl., Belgravia Dd **11**
  „   rd., Pimlico Ab **13**
  „   rd., Shepherd's
  Bush .. .. .. Ac **11**
Belgrave-sq., Belgravia Dc**11**
  „   st., Belgravia Dd **11**
  „   st., Stepney Bb **14**
  „   st., S., Pimlico Ad **7**
  „   st., Upper and
  Lower, Pimlico .. Ad **7**
Belgravia .. .. Dc **11**
Bell-la., Wentworth-st. Cb **6**
  „ st., Edgware-rd. Cb **11**
Belsize-la., Hampstead Ab **10**
  „   pk. .. .. Aa **4**
  „   Pk.-rd., Hmpstd. Ab**10**
  „   rd., Kilburn .. Ac **10**
  „   sq., Hampstead Ab **10**
Belvedere-rd., Lambeth Ba**13**
Bemerton-st., Islington Dc **10**
Bentinck-st., M'nchstr.-sq. Ac**8**
Benwell-rd., Holloway Db **10**
Benyon-rd., Kingsland Bc **9**
Beresford-rd., Highbury Bb **9**
  „   st., Walworth Bc **13**
Berkeley-sq., Mayfair Ab **7**
  „   st., Piccadilly Bb **7**
Bermondsey and st. .. Cb **13**
  „   N. Road Cb **13**
  „   station .. Cb **4**
  „   Wall .. Da **13**
Bernard-st., Commer.-rd. Db**6**
  „   Brunswk.-sq. Cb**8**
Berners-st., Oxford-st. Bc **8**
Berwick-st., Soho .. Ba **7**

Bessboro'gh-st., Pimlico Ab **13**
Bethlehem Hos., L'mb'h Bb**13**
Bethnal-green .. Ea **6**
  „   Junc. sta. Ca **4**
  „   rd. .. Cd **9**
Bethnal Green Museum Cd **9**
Betts-st., St George's in
  the East .. .. Ec **6**
Bevenden-st., Hoxton Bc **9**
Bevis Marks, St Mary Axe Cb **6**
Bickerton-rd., Holloway Ca**10**
Billingsgate Market .. Cc **6**
Billiter-st., Fenchurch-st. Cc **6**
Bird-st., Wapping .. Ed **6**
Birdcage-w., St James-p. Bc**7**
Bishop's-rd., Camberwell Bc**13**
  „   rd., Fulham .. Bb **12**
  „   rd., Paddington Cb**11**
  „   rd., Victoria-pk. Dc**9**
  „   Road station Aa **4**
Bishopsgate-st. .. Cb **6**
  „   st. station Ca **4**
Blackfriars Bridge .. Ac **6**
  „   Bridge sta. Bb **4**
  „   rd... .. Ad **6**
  „   station Bb **4**
Blackman-st., Southw'rk Ca**13**
Blackstock-rd., Highbury Ba**9**
Blackwall .. .. Cc **14**
  „   lane, Blackwall Dc**14**
  „   Entrance to
  South Dock .. .. Cc **14**
Blackwell Reach .. Dd**14**
Blakesley-st., Shadwell Ec **6**
Blandford-sq., Mrylebn. Db**11**
  „   st., Baker-st. Ac **8**
Blenheim-cres., Kensing-
  ton-park .. .. Bb **11**
Blind School, Lamb'th-rd. Ed**7**
  „   Southwark Bb **13**
Blomfield-rd., Maida-hll. Cb**11**
  „   st., Finsbury Cb **6**
Bloomfield-rd., Bow .. Cb **14**
  „   st., Bow Com. Cb**14**
  „   st., Dalston Cc **9**
Bloomsbury-sq. .. Cc **8**
  „   st. .. Cc **8**
Blue Anchor-rd. .. Db**13**
Blundell-st., Caledon-rd. Db**10**
Blurton-rd., Clapton .. Db **9**
Blythe-rd., Kensington Ad **11**
Bolingbroke-rd., Prim-
  rose-hill .. .. Bc **10**
Bolingbroke-rd., Shep-
  herd's Bush .. .. Ac **11**
Bolsover-st., Gt. Portd.-st. Bb**8**
Bolt-st., Deptford .. Be **14**
Bolton-row, Mayfair .. Ab **7**
  „ st., Ken'gton-pk. Bc**13**
  „ st., Piccadilly .. Bb **7**
Boltons, New Brompton Ca **12**
Bond-st., Chelsea .. Ca **12**
  „   Kennington Ac **13**
  „   Pentonville Da **8**
  „   Waterloo-rd. Dc **7**
  „   New and Old Bb **7**
Bonner's-la., Bethnal-gr. Dc **9**
  „   rd., Victoria-pk. Dc **9**

Bookham-st., Hoxton Bc **9**
Booth-st., Spitalfields Db **6**
Borough-rd., Southwark Bb**13**
  „   rd. station .. Cb **4**
Boston-st., Hackney .. Cc **9**
  „   Park-road Db **11**
Boundary-la., Walworth Cc **13**
  „   rd. Ac**10**
Bouverie-st., Fleet-st. Eb **7**
Bow Cb**14**
  „   Church, Cheapside Bc **6**
  „   Common-lane .. Cb**14**
  „   rd. Cb**14**
  „   st., Covent-garden Cb **7**
Bowling Green-la., Clerkl. Eb**8**
Brady-st., Whitechapel Eb **6**
Bramber-rd., M. End Ba **12**
Bramley-rd. Ab**11**
Brandon-st., Newington Cb**13**
Brecknock-rd. .. .. Cb **10**
Brewer-st., Golden-sq. Bb **7**
  „   Pimlico .. Bd **7**
Brewery-rd., C'l'd'nia-rd. Cb**10**
Brick-lane, Spitalfields Db **6**
  „ st., Piccadilly .. Ac **7**
Bricklayers Arms station Cb **4**
Bride-st., Liverpool-rd. Db**10**
Bridewell-pl., N. B'dge-st. Eb**7**
Bridge-rd., Battersea Cb **12**
  „   rd., Hammers'th Aa**12**
  „   rd., Limehouse Cc **14**
  „   st., Greenwich Ce **14**
  „   st., Mile End Bb **14**
  „   st., Westminster Cc **7**
Bridgewater-ho., Gn.-pk. Bc**7**
Bridport-pl. Hoxton Bc **9**
Bright-st. Poplar .. Cb **14**
Brighton-rd., St'keNewn Bb**9**
  „ st., Gray'sInn-rd. Da **8**
British Art Gallery .. Ab **13**
British Museum .. Cc**8**
Britton-st., Chelsea .. Ca **12**
Brixton-rd. .. .. Bc **13**
Broad-st., Bloomsbury Cc **8**
  „   Liverpool-st. Cb **6**
  „   Soho .. Bb **7**
  „   Wapping .. Ed **6**
  „   station .. Ca **4**
Bro'dhurst-gar. Hampd. Ab**10**
Broadwalk, The, Kensi. Cc **11**
Bro'dWalk, Regent's-pk. Aa**8**
  „ Wall, Blackfriars Ec **7**
  „ Sanctuary, W'stm'r Cc**7**
Broadway, Westminster Bc **7**
Broke-rd., Dalston .. Cc **9**
Bromley.. .. .. Cb**14**
  „   st., Stepney Bb **14**
Brompton-cres. .. Ca **12**
  „   Old and New Ca**12**
  „   rd. .. .. Cd **11**
  „   sq. Dc**11**
  „   station .. Ab **4**
Brondesbury station .. Aa **4**
Brook-gr. & rd. H'm's'th. Aa**12**
  „ st., Kennington-rd. Ed**7**
  „ st., Mayfair .. Ab **7**
  „ st., Stepney .. Bc**14**

Chester-sq., Pimlico .. Ad 7
,, st., Belgravia Ad 7
,, st., Greenwich Dd14
,, st., Kenngtn-rd. Bb13
,. ter., Pimlico Ad 7
,, ter., Reg'nts-pk. Aa8
Chesterfield-ho., Mayfair Ab7
Chestert'n-rd.,Not'g-hillAb11
Chetwynd-st.,Dart.-pk. Ca10
Cheyne-walk, Chelsea Cb 12
Chicksand-st., Spitalfids. Db6
Chipenh'm-rd.,Haro'-rd. Bb11
Children's Home, Higb'ry Bb9
Chilton-st., Deptford Bd 14
Chisenhale-rd.,Vict.-pk. Dc9
Chiswell-st.,Finsbury-sq. Bb6
Chrisp-st., Poplar .. Cb 14
ChristChurch,Victoria-st. Bd7
,, Kennigt'n-rd. Dd7
Christian-st.,Commer.-rd.Dc6
Christ'sHos.,Newgate-st. Ab6
Chryssell-rd., Brixton Bb 13
Church-la., Whitechapel Db6
,, rd., Battersea Cb 12
,, rd., Islington Bc 9
,, rd. Stoke-Newn. Cb 9
,, row, H'mpstead Ab10
,, rd., Homerton Db 9
,, row,St'keNewm. Bb9
,, st., Bl'ckfriars-rd. Ad6
,, st., Borough .. Bd 6
,, st., Chelsea .. Ca 12
,, st., Clapham-rd. Bc13
,, st., Deptford Ce 14
,, st.,Edgware-rd. Cb 11
,, st., Greenwich Ce 14
,, st., Kensington Bc11
,, st., Lambeth Bb13
,, st., Rotherhithe Ac14
,, st., Spitalfields Db 6
,, st., Waterloo-rd. Dc7
Churchhill-st.,Dart.-pk. Ca 10
Circus-rd.,Havers'k-hill Bb10
,, StJohn's-wd. Ac10
City of London Union Db 9
,, rd.. .. .. .. Bc 9
,, rd.-basin .. .. Bc 9
,, Temple, Holborn Ab 6
,, Union Workhouse,
Bow Cb14
Civil Service Commission,
Westminster .. .. Cc 7
Clapham Dc12
,, rd., Clapham Bc 13
Clapton-rd. .. .. Ca 9
Clare Market, Strand Da 7
Claremont-sq., Pent'nville Da8
Clarendon-rd.,Not'g-hill Bc11
,, sq., Somers-tn Ca8
,, st., Somers-tn. Ba8
,, st.,Walworth Cb13
Clarence-gds., R'g't's-pk. Bb8
,, rd.,K'ntish-tn.Cb10
,, rd., L. Clapton Cb9
,, rd., Mile End Ec9
,, rd., Old Ford Ca 14
,, st.,R'th'rhithe Bc14
Clarges-st., Mayfair .. Ab 7

Clark-st., Mile End .. Eb 6
Claverton-st., Pimlico Ab 13
Clayton-st., Kennington Bc13
Clement's Inn, Strand Da 7
Cleopatra's Needle, Vic-
toria Embankment Db 7
Clephane-rd., Islington Bb 9
Clerkenwell-green, E.C. Aa 6
,, rd., E.C. .. Aa 6
Cleveland-rd., Islington Bc 9
,, row, Pall Mall Bc 7
,, st.,Fitzroy-sq. Bb8
Clifden-rd., L. Clapton Db 9
Clifford's Inn, Fleet-st. Da 7
Clifford-st., NewBond-st. Bb7
Clifton-gr. &rd., Peckh'mDc13
,, rd.,Maida-vale Cb 11
,, rd., Marylebone Cb11
,, rd.,StJohn's-wd. Ac10
,, rd., New Cross Be 14
,, st., Finsbury .. Cb 6
Clinton-rd.,MileEnd-rd. Bb14
Clipstone-st.,Portland-pl. Bb8
Coal Exch., L. Thames-st.Cc6
Cobett's-la., R'therhithe Bd14
Coborn-rd., Mile End Dd 9
,, New-rd.OldFord Dc9
,, st., Mile End Ed 9
Cobourg-row, Pimlico Bd 7
Cockspur-st.,CharingCr'sCb7
ColdBath-sq., Clerkenwl. Db8
Coldhawk-rd., Shepherd's
Bush .. .. .. Ac 11
Colehill-lane, Fulham Bb 12
Coleman-st., Hoxton Bc 9
,, LondonWallBb6
Coleshill-st., Pimlico Da 12
College-cres.,Hampst'd Ab10
College of Surgeons,
Lincoln's Inn .. Da 7
College-pl., Chelsea .. Da 12
,, st.,Belvedere-rd. Dc7
,, st., Chelsea .. Ca 12
Collier-st., King's Cross Da 8
Collingham-rd.,Br'mpt'nCa12
Collingw'd-st., B'thnal-gr. Ea6
,, B'ckfriars-rd.Ec7
ColonialOffice,W'stm'st'r. Cc7
Columbia-rd., H'ckn'y-rd. Cc9
Commercial Docks,
Rotherhithe .. .. Bc 14
Commercial-rd.,Lamb'thDb7
,, rd., P'khamDc13
,, rd., Water-
loo-rd. .. .. .. Ba 13
Commercial-rd., East Eb 6
,, Sale-rooms,
Mark-lane .. .. Cc 6
Commercial-rd., East,
Stepney .. .. Bc 14
Comm'rcial-st., Rotherh. Bd14
,, Spitalfields Db6
Compton-st.,Regent-sq. Cb 8
,, Islington Ab 9
Conduit-st., Regent-st. Bb 7
CongressHall,L.Clapton Db9
Connaught-sq. Db11
Constitution Hill .. Ac 7

Cook's-rd., Walworth Bc 13
Copenhagen-st.,Isli'gt'nDc10
Copperas-la., Deptford Ce 14
Cornhill .. .. .. Bc 6
CornExchange,Mark-la. Cc6
Cork-st.,Burlington-gds. Bb7
Cornwall-gds., K'nsi'gt'nCa12
,, rd.,Waterl.-rd.Ba13
,, rd. .. Bb 11
Corporat'n-row,Clerkw'l. Eb8
Corunna-rd.,S.LambethAc13
Cottage-cr.,MileE'd-rd. Bb14
Cotton-st., Poplar .. Bb 14
Coulston-st.,Whitech'pel Db6
Covent Garden Market Cb 7
Coventry-st.,Bethnal-gr. Ea6
,, Leic'st'r-sq. Cb7
Cow Cross-st., Smithfield Ab6
Crab Tree Shott-rd.,
Peckham Dc13
Cranbo'rn-st., Leic'str-sq.Cb7
Cranbrook-st., Bethn'l-gr. Dc9
Cranmer-rd.,Brixton-rd.Bc13
Craven-hill, Bayswater Cc 11
,, rd., Paddington Cb11
,, st., Strand .. Cb 7
,, ter., Bayswater Cc11
Crawford-st.,M'ryleb'neDb11
Cremorne-gds., Chelsea Cb12
Cremorne New-rd. .. Cb12
Crescent-pl.,Morn'gtn-cr.Ba8
Cresse-st., Tot.Court.rd. Bc8
Crispin-st., Spitalfields Cb 6
Criterion Theatre, Picca. Bb7
Cromer-st.,Gray'sInn-rd. Cb8
Cromwell-rd.,S.Knsigtn.Ca12
Croom'sHill,Greenwich De14
CrosbyHall,Bishopgte-st.Cb6
Crosier-st., Lambeth Bb 13
Cross-st., Blackfriars-rd. Ec 7
,, Islington .. Ac 9
,, Leather-lane Ec 8
,, Southwark Bd 6
Crown-rd., Fulham .. Bb12
Crowndale-rd.,Cmdn-tn.Cc10
Crutched Friars .. Cc 6
Cubitt-st., Cubitt-tn. Dd 14
,, Town-pier ..Dd 14
,, town, I. of Dogs Cd14
Culford-rd., Kingsland Bc 9
Culvert-rd., Battersea Db 12
Cumberl'd Mkt.,Reg-pk. Ba8
,, st., Pimlico Da 12
,, ter.,Regt.-pk. Aa8
Cumming-st., Penton-
ville-rd .. .. Da 8
Cursitor-st.,Chancery-la. Dc8
Curzon-st., Mayfair .. Ab 7
Custom House & Quay Cc 6
Czar-st., Deptford .. Ce 14
D-street, Kensal-green Ba 11
Dacre-st., Pimlico .. Bd 7
Daisy-lane, Fulham .. Bc 12
Dalston .. .. .. Cb 9
,, lane, Dalston .. Gb 9
,, Junction station Ca 4
Dame-st., Islington .. Bc 9
Darnley-rd. W.,Hackney Db9

King Henry's-rd., Hampstead .. .. Bb 10
King Henry's-rd., K'gsld. Bb 9
   „ William-st., Greenwich .. .. Ce 14
King William-st., London-bridge .. .. Bc 6
King William-st., Strand Cb 7
Kings-rd., Camden-tn. Cc 10
   „ rd., Chelsea .. Ca 12
   „ rd., Fulham .. Bb 12
   „ rd., Hackney Wick Db 9
   „ rd., Kingsland .. Bb 9
   „ rd. W., Chelsea Cb 12
   „ College, Strand Db 7
   „ College-road .. Ab 10
   „ Cross .. .. Ca 8
   „ Cross rd... .. Da 8
   „ Cross station .. Ba 4
Kingsland .. .. Bb 9
   „ road .. .. Bc 9
Kingsgate-st., H. Holborn Dc 8
Kirby-st., Hatton-garden. Ec 8
Knapp-rd., Bromley .. Cb 14
Knightrider-st., St Paul's Bc 6
Knightsbridge, H'de-pk. Dc 11
L-street, Kensal-green Ba 11
Ladbroke-gr., Ntng.-hill Bb 11
   „ Grove-road, Notting-hill .. .. Bb 11
Ladbroke-rd., Nting.-hill Bc 11
   „ rd. station .. Aa 4
   „ sq., Nting.-hill Bc 11
Lady Lakes-gr., Mile End Eb 6
Lamb-lane, London-flds. Cc 9
Lambeth .. .. Bb 13
   „ Bridge .. Bb 13
   „ LowMarsh, Lm. Dc 7
   „ Palace, Lmbh. Bb 13
   „ Pal'ce-rd., L'm. Bb 13
   „ rd., Lambeth Bb 13
   „ sq., Lambeth Dc 7
   „ st., Goodman's-fields .. .. .. Dc 6
Lambeth-walk, Lamb'th Bb 13
   „ Workhouse, Newington .. .. Bb 13
Lamb's Conduit-st. .. Db 8
Lancaster-gate, H'd.pk., Cc 11
   „ rd., Hampstd. Ab 10
   „ rd., Kensington-pk. .. .. Bb 11
Lancaster-road W. .. Ab 11
   „ st., Southw'rk Ba 13
Lancing-st., Euston-sq. Ca 8
Langdon-rd., Up. Hl'wy. Ca 10
Langham-pl., Regent-st., Bc 8
   „ st., Marylebone Bc 8
Lansdowne-house, Berkeley-sq. .. .. Ab 7
Lansdowne-rd., Dalston Cc 9
   „ pl. and rd., South Lambeth .. Ac 13
Lansdowne-rd., Notting-hill .. .. Bc 11
Landseer-st., Battersea Db 12
Latchmere-grove, Btsea. Dc 12
   „ rd., Batt'rsea Dc 12

Latimer-road .. .. Ab 11
   „ rd. station .. Aa 4
Lauriston-rd., Hackney Dc 9
Lavender-grove, Dalston Cc 9
   „ hill, Battersea Dc 12
   „ rd., Battersea Cc 12
Lawn-rd., Haverst'k-hill Bb 10
Laystall-st., Gray's Inn-road .. .. .. Db 8
Lea, River .. .. Eb 9
   „ Bridge-rd., Clapton Da 9
Leadenhall Market .. Cc 6
   „ st. .. .. Cc 6
Leader-st., Chelsea .. Ca 12
Leather-lane, Holborn Ec 8
Ledbury-rd., Not'g-hill Bb 11
Lee-st., Kingsland-rd. Cc 9
Lefevre-rd., Old Ford Ec 9
Leicester-sq. .. .. Cb 7
Leigh-st., Burton-cres. Cb 8
Leighton-rd., K'ntish-tn. Cb 10
Leinster-sq., Bayswater Bb 11
   „ ter., Bayswater Cb 11
Leipsic-rd., Camberwell Cc 13
Leman-st., Whitechapel Dc 6
   „ st. station .. Cb 4
Lenthall-rd., Ki'gsl'nd-rd. Cc 9
Lever-st., City-road .. Bd 9
Lexham-gds., Cr'mwl-rd. Ba 12
Libra-rd., Old Ford .. Ec 9
Licensed Victuallers' Asylum .. .. Dc 13
Lillie-rd., Chelsea .. Ba 12
Lime-st., Fenchurch-st. Cc 6
Limehouse .. .. Bc 14
   „ Basin .. Bc 14
   „ Causeway Cc 14
   „ Cut .. Cb 14
   „ Cut Entran. Bc 14
   „ dock & pier Bc 14
   „ Reach .. Bc 14
Lincoln-st., Mile End Bb 14
Lincoln's Inn .. .. Dc 8
   „ Fields .. Dc 8
Linsey-rd., Bermondsey Db 13
Linton-st., NewNorth-rd. Bc 9
Lisle-st., Leicester-sq. Cb 7
Lismore-rd., Kentish-tn. Bb 10
Lisson-grove, N., Maryl. Db 11
   „ st., Marylebone Db 11
Litchfield-rd. .. .. Bb 14
   „ st., Soho .. Cb 7
Little Britain, Aldersgate Ab 6
   „ Cambridge-st., Hackney-rd. .. Cc 9
Little Chelsea .. .. Ca 12
   „ Newport-st., Soho Cb 7
   „ Pulteney-st., Soho Bb 7
   „ Queen-st., Lincoln's Inn .. Dc 8
Little St James' st., St J.-st. Bc 7
   „ Tower-hill, Tower Dc 6
Liverpool-rd., Holloway Db 10
   „ st., Bshpsgt.-st. Cb 6
   „ st., King's Cross Ca 8
   „ st., Walworth Cb 13
   „ st. station .. Ca 4
Lloyd-sq., Pentonville Da 8

Lloyd's-row, St J'n st.-rd. Eb 8
Lock Hosp., Wstbrn.-gr. Bb 11
Lock's Fields .. .. Cb 13
Loddige-rd., Hackney Cc 9
Lombard-rd., Battersea Cb 12
   „ st. .. .. Bc 6
London Bridge .. Bc 6
   „ Docks .. .. Dc 6
   „ Bridge station Cb 4
   „ Fields, Hackney Cc 9
   „ Fields station Ca 4
   „ Hospital .. Eb 6
   „ Missionary Soc., Bloomfield-st. .. Cb 6
London-rd., Deptford Bd 14
   „ rd., Greenwich Ce 14
   „ rd., Southwark Bb 13
   „ rd., Up. Clapton Cb 9
   „ st., Paddington Cb 11
   „ st., Tot. Court-rd. Bb 8
   „ Wall .. .. Bb 6
Long Acre .. .. Cb 7
   „ lane, Bermondsey Ca 13
   „ lane, Smithfield Ab 6
Longford-st., R'g'nt's-pk. Bb 8
Lord's Cricket ground Ca 11
Lorrimore-rd. and st. Bc 13
Lothbury, Bank .. Bb 6
Lothian-rd., Camberwell Bc 13
Loudoun-rd., St J'n's-wd. Ac 10
   „ rd. station .. Aa 4
Love-lane, Shadwell Bc 14
Lower Berkeley-st., Manchester-sq. .. .. Ac 8
Lower-rd., Rotherhithe Bd 14
   „ Clapton .. Db 9
   „ Clapton-rd. .. Cb 9
   „ E. Smithfield, St Katherine Docks .. Dd 6
Lower George-st., Chels. Da 12
   „ Grosvenor-gdns., Pimlico .. .. Ad 7
Lower Grosvenor-pl., Pimlico .. .. Ad 7
Lower Heath, Hampstd. Aa 10
   „ Holloway .. Db 10
   „ Kennington-lane Bb 13
   „ Que'n-st., R'hithe. Bc 14
   „ Richmond-rd., Putney .. .. Ac 12
Lower Seymour-st., Portman-sq. .. .. Ac 8
Lower Sloane-st., Chels. Da 12
   „ Thames-st. .. Cc 6
Lowndes-pl., Belgravia Ad 7
   „ sq., Belgravia Dc 7
   „ st., Belgravia Dd 11
Lucas-st., Shadwell .. Bc 14
Lucey-rd., Bermondsey Db 13
Ludgate Circus .. Ab 6
   „ Hill .. .. Ab 6
   „ Hill station .. Bb 4
Luke-st., Finsbury .. Ca 6
   „ Spitalfields .. Da 6
Lunatic Asylum, Bthl.-gr. Cd 9
Lupus-st., Pimlico .. Ab 13
Lyall-st., Pimlico .. Ad 7
Lyceum Theatre, Strand Db 7